RARE POEMS

RARE POEMS

OF

THE SEVENTEENTH CENTURY

Chosen & Edited by

L. BIRKETT MARSHALL

M.A., Ph.D.

CAMBRIDGE

AT THE UNIVERSITY PRESS

1936

CAMBRIDGE
UNIVERSITY PRESS

University Printing House, Cambridge CB2 8BS, United Kingdom

Published in the United States of America by Cambridge University Press, New York

Cambridge University Press is part of the University of Cambridge.

It furthers the University's mission by disseminating knowledge in the pursuit of
education, learning and research at the highest international levels of excellence.

www.cambridge.org
Information on this title: www.cambridge.org/9781107418219

© Cambridge University Press 1936

First published 1936
First paperback edition 2014

A catalogue record for this publication is available from the British Library

ISBN 978-1-107-41821-9 Paperback

CONTENTS

〈 v 〉

INTRODUCTION

In his general introduction to the *Minor Poets of the Caroline Period* Mr George Saintsbury wrote:

> From the point of view of literary history, and not from that point only, the neglect of minorities is a serious and may be fatal mistake.... Every fresh example may, it may almost be asserted that every fresh example does, give the rule with a difference; and by far the larger number of these differences are at least illustrative. From the confinement of the attention to a few examples, however brilliant and famous, come hasty generalisation and insufficient exposition, not seldom downright errors.

By means of this collection of very rare seventeenth-century verse I have tried to give some more worthy and distinctive minor poetry to the English Anthology and to add to our knowledge of what has been, surely, up to the present time, the greatest period of such poetry in our literature.

These poems, about two hundred in number, are a selection made from the numerous verses which I have met with while wandering along the very unfrequented by-paths of the seventeenth century. Very few indeed of them have previously appeared in modern anthologies of the poetry of that period. Yet in almost every case the poems have been chosen for some poetic merit. In no case, I think, can I be accused of selecting a poem merely for some obscure interest.

Most of the poems have come from rare, often hitherto unknown, neglected, printed volumes of poetry. Many of the latter were issued by their authors and have never been reprinted. A number exist in one single copy. But while reading MSS. in the British Museum and the Bodleian

Libraries I have occasionally found some poems which have been overlooked by collectors and which are, nevertheless, worthy of a reprint. I have also included at the end a few anonymous poems which have never appeared in any modern anthology.

In all poems I have somewhat modernized the punctuation. The spelling of the texts, except for an obvious printer's error, I have left severely alone. In the few obscure passages, of course, there has very infrequently been a choice of reading.

I am deeply indebted to Mr John Drinkwater for introducing me to some of these poets.

L. BIRKETT MARSHALL

Enfield and
Oxford
October, 1936

RARE POEMS

OF THE SEVENTEENTH CENTURY

ASHMORE

JOHN ASHMORE (*fl.* 1621). The only book which bears his name is *Certain Selected Odes of Horace, Englished... Whereunto are added sundry new Epigrammes, Anagrammes, Epitaphes*, 1621. Contents are interesting historically since they are some of the earliest translations of Horace's *Odes* into English. There is a certain charm about this original Epitaph. In spite of conventional subject-matter and language there is a sad sincerity. The plaintive burden is especially pleasing.

AN EPITAPH UPON THE
DEATH OF ELISABETH BRIGGES, DAUGHTER TO
THE DISCREET MATRON AND WIDOW,
BETTRICE BRIGGES

COME, Virgins, come! why doe you linger so,
  With streams of tears that from your swol'n eyes
   show'r?
Her Grave with Roses and with Lillies strowe
 That of your Garland was the fairest flower.
   Lillies and Roses soon decay and perish,
   While bitter Worm-wood and sharp Nettles flourish.

Your Garlands break! henceforth no garlands bear;
 Their fading doth your fading state express.
For Garlands, deadly Yeugh and Elder weare,
 And branches of the saddest Cyparesse.
   Lillies and Roses etc.

Ashmore   Ye Holly-hocks, why hold you downe your heads?
        And violets, why pine you so away?
    Because (alas!) that shee from you is fled,
        That drest you and hath ta'ne her leave for aye?
           Lillies etc.

    O Hymen, why didst thou pale Death permit,
        Within thy Right to set his hatefull feet,
    And take her, that for thy sweet Rites was fit,
        For Bridals that gave her a Winding sheet?
           Lillies etc.

    When Death arrested her with his sad Mace,
        And cloudy Mists her Senses over-spread,
    Her native favour he could not disgrace,
        Which was compos'd of purest white and red.
           Lillies etc.

    All that thy sweet conditions did know,
        Desired that their lives they so might spend:
    And all that from this life did see thee goe,
        Desired that their lives they so might end.
           Lillies and Roses soon decay and perish,
           While bitter Worm-wood and sharp Nettles flourish.

Certain Selected Odes of Horace,
Englished, 1621

EX M. ANTONIO FLAMINIO,   *Ashmore*
AD AGELLUM SUUM. SIC INCIPIT,
"UMBRAE FRIGIDULAE..."

COOL Shades, Air-fanning Groves,
    With your soft Whisperings,
    Where Pleasure smiling roves
Through deawie Caves and Springs,
And bathes her purple Wings:

With Flowrs-inamel'd Ground,
(Nature's fair Tapestry),
Where chattering Birds abound,
Flickring from tree to tree
With change of Melody:

Sweet Liberty and Leasures,
Where still the Muses keep,
O! if to those true Treasures
That from your Bosome peep,
I might securely creep:

If I might spend my dayes,
(Remote from publicke brawls),
Now tuning lovely Laies,
Now light-foot Madrigals,
N'er checkt with sudden calls:

Now follow Sleep that goes
Rustling i'th green-wood Shade;
Now milk my goat, that knowes,
(With her young fearfull Cade),
The pail i'th cooly Glade;

⟨ 3 ⟩   I-2

And with Boals fil'd to th' Brims
Of milky Moisture new,
To water my dry'd Lims,
And t'all the wrangling Crew
Of Cares to bid Adew;

What life then should I lead!
How like then would it bee
Unto the Gods, that tread
Ith' starry Gallery
Of true Felicity!

But you, O Virgins sweet,
In Helicon that dwell,
That oft the Fountains greet,
When you the Pleasures tell
Ith' Country that excell:

If I my life, though dear,
For your far dearer sake,
To yeeld would nothing fear,
From Citee's tumults take mee
And free i'th Country make mee.

Ibid.

BARKSDALE

CLEMENT BARKSDALE (1609–1687). Author of numerous religious works, translations from Grotius, sermons and a few verses. Like many other clerics of the century he published a solitary volume of verses. This was *Nympha Libethris; or the Cotswold Muse*, 1651.

DEDICATION OF
PART THREE OF NYMPHA LIBETHRIS
TO MY NEPHEW, J. B.

THE care thy Father once bestow'd on me,
   I very gladly would return to thee.
   What I to thee, (thus love in a blood runs),
Do thou communicate unto my sons.
I have no land to give, such is my chance,
Take this poetical inheritance.
A little here is best: because much more
Of poetry, perhaps, would make you poor.

Nympha Libethris; or the
Cotswold Muse, 1651

UPON THE DECEASE OF MY INFANT LADY

E'EN so, the nipping wind in May doth come,
And blast the choicest fruit in the first bloom:

Yet shall this Blossom of Nobility,
Preserv'd by angels' care, immortal be.

Such delicate bodies sleep, and are laid by
In their repositories. They do not die.

Ibid.

BARON

ROBERT BARON (*fl.* 1645). His first printed work, *Erotopaig-nion, or the Cyprian Academy*, is dated "from my chambers in Gray's Inn", 1647. It is dedicated to James Howell, who praised it in *Epistolae Ho-Elianae*. Many poems in it were stolen directly from Milton. His other volume of verses was entitled *Pocula Castalia*, 1650. He also wrote a tragedy, *Mirʒa*.

SONNET

TO ELIZA UPON MAY DAY MORNING, 1649

S EE, Fairest! Virgins gather dew;
Wing'd Heralds blaze on every bough;
May's come; if you say so, 'tis true.
For thus your Power's 'bove his that seasons sway,
He brings the Moneth, but you must make it May.
Arise, Arise,
Bright eyes,
And silver over Beautie's skies:
You set, Noon's Night: you up, each Day
Turns jolly May.

Now Venus hatches her young Doves,
This fruitful Moneth's proper for Loves,
Though Aprill sayes like her it moves
Full of sad change; but you may chase away
All showres with smiles, and make all our days May.
Arise, Arise, etc.

All but you love, (though all love you),
The Birds their song each morn renew,
Even Earth has don'd her gaudy hue.

Since all things else are blith, let your kind Ray   *Baron*
Do more than Sol's, and make in me too May.
        Arise, Arise, etc.

   May this Moneth last; when bald Time shall
    Climb your fair Hill of Youth, may all
    His steps be slip'rie, and he back fall
To Beautie's Spring, that your cheek may alway
That lustre weare that now adorneth May.
        Arise, Arise, etc.

Pocula Castalia, 1650

SONG

THE ROSE

FROM Eliza's Breast,
    (That sweet Nest
    Where my heart and Cupid rest),
I took a Rose-bud, which flew thither
For shelter from the droughty weather.

   Whilst a place it held
     In that field
   Of Lillies with Violet Mazes rill'd,
It gathered all its sweetnesse there
And smells, not of it selfe, but Her.

   I thought to kisse the
     Stalk, but see
   It, angry, raiz'd its fangs at me,
And prickt my lips in poor revenge
For making it its sweet bed change.

Baron   Whilst it therein laid,
                In its shade
           Thousand Cupids frisk'd and plai'd
With Fairy Graces thither come
To prove her Breast Elizium.

           Whence had it this die?
                Did the skie
           Lend it her Ruby Livery?
No, No, it only blusht to see
Her cheeks excell its gallantry.

           See! so to be sham'd
                And be tane
           From her bosom, the poor wan
Languishing floure its leaves hath spred
For Griefe, and lies, (griefe's Martyr), dead.

           In it yet doth lie
                Fragrancy:
           Thus must choycest Beauties die;
But, as this, after death shall be
Still od'rous in their memory.

                                      Ibid.

TO ELIZA,
WITH A TULIP FASHION'D WATCH

LADY,
This measure of Time accept with serene eye
From him whose Love to you shall Time out-vie.
See! what disguise this spie of Day doth wear;
A Tulip! as the forge its Garden were.
Indeed heat procreates even Flowers, but this
A peece of an Egyptian Mysterie is.

Time, by a Flower, denotes how suddenly   *Baron*
Earth's frailer crops bloom, flourish, fade and die.
In speciall Beauty, (that sweet Tulip), hasts
To waite on Time: then use it whilst it lasts.
    When these small clicking orbs you busie hear
Panting in their round journey, like the Spheres,
Think so my constant heart doth palpitate
Towards you, and th'Pulse of my Affections beat,
N'er to stand till shee that each happy thing
Envies, (the peevish sister), cuts the string.

Ibid.

BEEDOME

THOMAS BEEDOME (d. 1640?). Author of a single volume of verse, *Poems Divine and Humane*, which was published post-humously in 1641 by Henry Glapthorne, the minor dramatist and poet. Beedome is one of the most interesting and capable of the lesser poets of the century. There are lapses and grotes-que "conceits", but, as a close imitator of Donne, he sometimes reaches the heights. At moments he achieves violent, startling, impassioned utterance: often he finds a vigorous thought and vigorous words to express it.

LOVES APOSTASY TO HIS FRIEND MR E. D.

TUT, let her goe; can I endure all this,
 Yet dye to doate upon a Mayden's kisse?
 Is there such Magicke in her lookes that can,
Into a foole transfigurate a man?
Didst thou not love her? true: and she disdaine
To meet thy vertue? let her meet her shame.
Were she as faire as she herselfe would be,
Adorn'd with all the cost of bravery;
Could she melt hearts of flint, and from her eye
Give her beholders powers to live or die;
I'de rather begge she would pronounce my death,
Then be her scorne, though that preserv'd my breath.
Rise heart! and be not fool'd: s'foote, what a shame
Were it for thee to re-incense one flame
From the declining sparke! dost thou not know
As shee's a woman, her whole sexe doth owe
To thine all honour? her false heart and pride
Dare not oppose thy faith? then turne high tyde,
And let her, since her scorne doth so disease thee,
By her repentance strive again to please thee.

Poems Divine and Humane, 1641

THE QUESTION AND ANSWER

Beedome

WHEN the sad ruines of that face
In its owne wrinkles buried lyes,
And the stiffe pride of all its grace,
By time undone, fals slack and dyes:
    Wilt thou not sigh, and wish in some vext fit,
    That it were now as when I courted it?

And when thy glasse shall it present,
Without those smiles which once were there,
Showing like some stale monument,
A scalpe departed from its haire,
    At thy selfe frighted wilt not start and sweare
    That I belied thee, when I call'd thee faire?

Yes, yes, I know thou wilt, and so
Pitty the weakenesse of thy scorne,
That now hath humbled thee to know,
Though faire it was, it is forlorne,
    Love's sweetes thy aged corps embalming not,
    What marvell if thy carkasse, beauty, rot?

Then shall I live, and live to be
Thy envie, thou my pitty; say
When e're thou see mee, or I thee,
(Being nighted from thy beautie's day),
    'Tis hee, and had my pride not wither'd mee,
    I had, perhaps, beene still as fresh as hee.

Then shall I smile, and answer: "True thy scorne
Left thee thus wrinkled, slackt, corrupt, forlorne."

Ibid.

I NEVER saw thee: but should grossely lie
 To say I know thee not, for silly I,
 Or one that is more stupid, may well guesse
At what thou art by what thou dost expresse.
Oh that blest day, when first my willing hand
Opt the remembrance of this Sinsicke land!
Trust me, I griev'd to thinke that now my age
Had sixteene summers acted on this stage,
Yet was a stranger to so rare a soule
As thine; whose heaven-bred boldnesse durst controle
Without respect of persons, every sinne,
That to thy knowledge had committed bin.
Then next thy Satyres, and thy Motto, I
Made hast to purchase, where I might espie
How some too base for earth, not worth a name,
Sought by their mire and dirt to clay thy fame.
And credit mee, I hardly could forbeare,
Upon these pittied lines to drop a teare.
But that I know vertue oppos'd by fate,
Lookes greatest, (like the Sunne), in lowest state:
When other wits, who have in some base rime
Implor'd of fate that they might conquer time,
Shall like those paper toyes, in which they trust,
Be eate by wormes, or molded into dust,
And want a name, thou, by thy vertues gract,
Shall live till earth by fire be imbract.

Ibid.

BEING A MEDITATION TO MY SELFE

WHY wouldst thou live, (fond soule), dost thou
    not know
    From whence thou cam'st, and whither thou
    must goe?
Can walls of clay so much thy sense delight,
As to debarre thee from that glorious flight
Which thou shouldst covet? canst thou idly prize
The mire that loads thy wings unfit to rise?
Shouldst thou still live, it were but still to see
Some new sceane Acted in thy Tragidie;
Thou couldst but do tomorrow as this day,
Commit fresh sinne, sleepe, eate, or drinke, and play.
No matter then how soone thou dye: then come,
Prepare thyselfe to waite thy Judge's dombe;
Thou cam'st from heav'n; then labour to draw neere
Thy quiet center. If thou once rest there,
Thy walls of clay, the mire that loads thy wings,
Shall be a mansion for the King of Kings.
Thy Tragedy shall end, thy sinne shall cease,
And thou rest ever in an endlesse peace.
Bee't when thou please, good God, at morne or noone,
So I die well, no matter, Lord, how soone.

Ibid.

EPITAPHIUM REGIS SWEDORUM

HEERE sleepes hee who was and is
The subject of eternall blisse.

Religion, and no other end,
Caus'd him his blood and means to spend.

He conquer'd all; onely his breath
He lost, by which he conquer'd death.

Now would'st thou know whom we deplore?
'Tis Sweden, Reader; hush, no more,

Lest while thou read, thou and this stone
Be both alike by death made one.

For death and griefe are neare of kinne,
So thou might'st die, being griev'd for him.

Cuius memoriae sacratae haec pie flevit: T.B.

Ibid.

TO THE NOBLE S^R. FRANCIS DRAKE

DRAKE, pererrati novit quem terminus orbis,
Et cuius faciem vidit uterque polus:
Si taceant homines facient te sydera notum,
Sol nescit comitis non memor esse sui.

Drake, who the world hast conquer'd like a scrole;
Who saw'st the Articke and Antarticke Pole;
If men were silent, starres would make thee knowne,
Phoebus forgets not his companion.

Ibid.

THE BROKEN HEART

Beedome

SONG

COUNT the sighs, and count the teares,
    Which have in part my budding yeares:
    Comment on my wofull looke,
Which is now blacke sorrow's booke.
Read how love is overcome,
Weepe and sigh, and then be dumbe.
Say it was your charity
To helpe him whose eyes are dry.
Here paint my Cleora's name,
Then a hart and then a flame;
Then marke how the heart doth fry
When Cleora is so nigh.
Though the flame did doe its part,
'Twas the name that broke the heart.
Peace, no more: no more you need
My sad history to read.
Fold the paper up agen,
And report to other men
These complaints can justly prove
Hearts may breake, that be in love.

Ibid.

SONG

COME sit thee downe, and with a mislyn charme
    Ceaze my incircled arme,
    Till lockt in fast imbraces wee discover
      In every eye a lover;
Then lost in that sweete extacy of blisses,
    Wee'le speake our thoughts in kisses,

In which wee'le melt our soules, and mixe them so,
That what is mine is thine; there's none shall know.

Rare mistery of love, and wonders too,
    Which none but wee can doe:
Nor shall the leaden spirits of all those
    Who speak of love in tamer prose
Beleeve our joys: but daily censure us,
    Onely for loving thus.
Ah! how I smile, that doubly blest, we doe
Injoy our selves, and all their envie too.

Ibid.

TO HIS MISTRESS,
WHEN SHEE WAS GOING INTO THE COUNTRY

YES, yes, it must be so, but must there be,
    When you depart, no memory had of mee?
    My soule being rack't as large a distance too
To meete you there, as I must be from you,
While the glad spring, for joy you shall be seene,
Meetes your approach, and cloaths her selfe in greene,
And the fresh morning to salute your rise,
Bedewes the ground from its o'rejoyed eyes;
(For joy, like griefe, we know, sometimes appeares
Writ on our cheekes, with characters of teares.)
Goe and be happy, goe, and when you see
The trusty Ivy claspe its much lov'd tree,
And with its amorous intwinings cover
The welcome waiste of its imbraced lover,
Thinke it our Embleme then, and prov'd to be
The happy shadow of my love and mee.
Goe and be happy, and, smooth as are thy lookes,

Show thee thy face; then let thy thoughts supply,   *Beedome*
And, though I be not, thinke that I am by:
For if the heart be taken for whole man,
I must be by thee, be thou where thou can.
Goe, and when pretty birds on some small spray
Neere to thy window welcome in the day,
Awake, and thinke, when their sweete notes you
    heare,
I was before-hand, and had sung them there.
Goe, and whate're thou chance to heare or see,
Be it bird, or brooke, or shade or tree,
If it delights thee, may my soule in it
Move thy true joyes under that counterfeit.
So, aske not how I doe when you are there,
For at your mercy well or ill I fare.
For now me thinkes my heart so high doth swell,
It must inforce a breath, farewell, farewell.

                                                    Ibid.

TO HIS MISTRESSE ON HER SCORNE

RESOLVE me, dearest, why two hearts in one
    Should know the sinne of separation.
    Must the sweete custome of our oft stolne kisses
Be lost, and we live empty of those blisses?
Or do the frownes of some old over-seer
Nourish thy feare, or make thy love lesse freer?
Why did'st thou suffer mee those sweetes to steale,
Which but thine own, no tongue can e're reveale,
And prompt mee to a daring, to beleeve
That my sad heart should find no cause to grieve,
Yet now at last hast mockt my hope so farre,
That I have met a cloud, though meant a starre?

Beedome   Well, take thy tryumph, study but to be
True to thy selfe, as thou art false to mee,
And thou shalt meet a conquest yet. When I
Have groan'd unto the world my Elegy
And thy unjust disdaine, perhaps I shall
Obtaine this honour in my funerall:
Thy poysonous guilt, mixt with thy perjur'd breath,
May make thee wither with mee unto death:
So shall I tryumph in my Ashes too,
In that my innocence hath conquer'd you,
And then my eye rejoyce, in that I have
Thy scorne, to be a mourner at my grave.

Ibid.

THE PETITION

HEARE mee, my God, and heare mee soone,
    Because my morning toucheth noone,
    Nor can I looke for their delight,
Because my noone layes hold on night:
I am all circle, my morne, night, and noone
Are individable; then heare mee soone.

Thou art all time my God, and I
Am part of that eternity:
Yet being made, I want that might
To be as thou art, Infinite:
As in thy flesh, so be thou Lord to mee,
That is, both infinite, and eternity.

But I am dust; at most, but man,
That dust extended to a span:
A span indeed, for in thy hand,

Stretcht or contracted, Lord, I stand;   *Beedome*
Contract and stretch mee too, that I may be
Straightn'd on earth, to be enlarg'd to thee.

But I am nothing; then how can
I call my selfe, or dust, or man?
Yet thou from nothing all didst frame,
That all things might exalt thy name,
Make mee but something, then, my God to thee;
Then shall thy praise be all in all to mee.

Ibid.

THE CHOYCE

WHAT care I though she be faire,—
Haire, snow-like hand, or Sun-like eye,
If in that beauty I not share,
Were she deformed, what care I?
What care I though she be foule,—
Haire, swarthy hand, or sunne-burnt eye,
So long as I enjoy her soule,
Let her be so, why, what care I?
Dimme sight is cosen'd with a glosse
Of gaudy gowne, or humerous haire;
Such gold in melting leave more drosse
Than some unpolish't pieces share.
Be she faire, or foule, or either,
Or made up of both together,
Be her heart mine, her hand or eye
Be what it will, why, what care I?

Ibid.

CHAMBERLAIN

ROBERT CHAMBERLAIN (1607, alive in 1662). His works
consist of a comedy, *The Swaggering Damsel*, 1640, jest-books
(containing poems and epigrams), broadsides, pamphlets and
an undergraduate book of verses. The latter is *Nocturnall
Lucubrations*, 1638 (reissued 1652).

TO HIS HONOURED FRIEND, MR GILES BALLE,
MERCHANT

ON THE SPRING

THE lofty Mountains standing on a row,
Which but of late were periwig'd with Snow,
Doff their old coats, and now are daily seene
To stand on tiptoes, all in swaggering greene.
Meadows and gardens are prankt up with buds,
And chirping birds now chant it in the woods.
The warbling Swallow, and the Larks do sing,
To welcome in the glorious, verdant Spring.

Nocturnall Lucubrations, 1638

IN PRAISE OF COUNTRY LIFE

THE winged fancies of the learned quill
Tell of strange wonders: sweet Parnassus' hill,
Castalia's well, the Heliconian spring,
Star-spangled valleys where the Muses sing.
Admired things another storie yeelds,
Of pleasant Tempe and th'Elysian fields;
Yet these are nothing to the sweet that dwells
In low-built cottages and country cells.

What are the scepters, thrones, and crownes of Kings,   *Chamberlain*
But gilded burdens and most fickle things?
What are great offices but cumbring troubles?
And what are honours but dissolving bubbles?
What though the gates of greatness be frequented
With chains of glittering gold? He that's contented
Lives in a thousand times a happier way
Than he that's tended thus from day to day.
Matters of state, nor yet domestick jars,
Comets portending death, nor blazing stars,
Trouble his thoughts: hee'l not post-haste run on
Through Lethe, Styx, and fiery Phlegiton
For gold or silver: he will not affright
His golden slumbers in the silent night
For all the pretious wealth or sumptuous pride
That lies by Tiber, Nile, or Ganges' side.
Th'imbroider'd meadows, and the crawling streams
Make soft and sweet his undisturbed dreams.
He revels not by day nor in the nights,
Nor cares he much for musical delights:
And yet his humble roofe maintains a quire
Of singing crickets round about the fire.
This harmless life he leads—and, dare I say,
Doth neither wish, nor fear, his dying day.

Ibid.

CHAMBERLAYNE

SIR JAMES CHAMBERLAYNE (1640–1699). Baronet of Wickham in Oxfordshire. Author of two very rare volumes of sacred verse: *A Sacred Poem, etc.* 1680, and *Manuductio ad Coelum, etc.* 1681. The latter was written "to promote holy desires in the sincere Christian". Few Christians could bear to read it now. Both poems are full of wretched stuff, in rhyming couplets, for the most part. But in front of the earlier work is this beautiful dedication, with the exquisite frankness of its third stanza.

DEDICATION

1

THIS little Book, my God and King,
The first fruits of my Muse, I bring
Unto thy throne, an Offering.

2

'Twould look more lovely, I confess,
Were it attir'd in the dress
Of abler Pens, than in my Verse;

3

But since my Numbers could not flow
In loftier Strains, than here they do,
For Reasons Thou and I do know;

4

Accept the Present; though it be
Too mean a gift for Majesty,
Lord, 'tis my All, and due to Thee.

A Sacred Poem, etc. 1680

COKAYNE

SIR ASTON COKAYNE (1608–1684). A good-natured, cheerful, Derbyshire squire who wrote plays and poems. His best-known play, which "diverted" Charles II, was *Trappolin, a supposed Prince*, 1658. This farcical comedy was often played, in adapted forms, during the eighteenth century. Cokayne was a friend of many literary figures of the time. His first volume of verses appeared in 1658 and was entitled, *Small poems of divers sorts*. Reissued five times, under varying titles, it contains a few poems of definite literary value, though all are artificial.

SONNET

D EAR saint, I do love you so well,
  You cannot think, nor I can tell.
  As when from earth some look on high
And see the hights that grace the skie,
They think them small, because they seem
Not unto them to be extreme;
So you perchance when you do read
My love dress'd in so poor a weed
As my weak Muse can frame, will straight
Or think it counterfeit, or light:
But could my hand express my mind,
You would no longer be unkinde;
For 'tis so full of love to you,
You cannot think, nor I can show.

Small poems of divers sorts, 1658

LADY, I do not give this Book alone,
But with't my heart, which you have made
        your own:
Censure my verses as you please; but be
Kind to my heart, lest you do ruine me.
I made these little Poems, and, (if you
Vouchsafe your love to me), you make me too.
Be kind as you are fair, I wish no other;
So make a doubtful man an happy Lover.

Ibid.

TO PLAUTIA

AWAY, fond Thing! tempt me no more!
    I'le not be won with all thy store!
    I can behold thy golden hair,
And for the owner nothing care:
Thy Starry eyes can look upon,
And be mine own when I have done;
Thy cherry, ruby lips can kiss,
And for fruition never wish:
Can view the Garden of thy cheeks,
And slight the roses there as leeks:
Can hear thee sing with all thine Art,
Without enthralling of mine heart:
My Liberty thou can'st not wrong
With all the Magick of thy tongue:
Thy warm Snow-breasts and I can see
And neither sigh nor wish for thee:
Behold thy feet, which we do bless
For bearing so much happiness,

⟨ 24 ⟩

Yet they at all should not destroy
My strong-preserved Liberty:
Could see thee naked, as at first
Our Parents were, when both uncurst,
And with my busy, searching eyes
View strictly thy hid rarities;
Yet, after such a free survey,
From thee no Lover go away.
For thou art false and wilt be so:
I else no other fair would woo.
Away, therefore, tempt me no more!
I'le not be won with all thy store.   *Ibid.*

OF A MISTRESS

I LOVE a lass as fair as ere was seen,
    Yet have I never seen if she be fair:
Grandees her suitors have and servants been,
    And they that wooe her now great Nobles are;
How can I, therefore, think that she will deign
To look on me? I fear I love in vain.

Unto the Beauty which I do so desire
    I will make haste, to see how fair she is;
And though I find my betters wooers by her,
    I will be bold, and all my thoughts express;
Which when I have done, will she, therefore, deign
To pity me? I fear I love in vain.

I'le tell her that her hairs are golden Twines
    Able t'enamour all the Deities;
And that her eyes are two celestial signs,
    More glorious than the twelve within the skies.
When I have told her this, will she then deign
To love me too? I fear I love in vain.

〈 25 〉

Cokayne   If, (when that I have said what I can say
               And made what Protestations I can make),
        She will be proud and coy, and say me Nay,
               Though ne'er so fair, my heart from her I'le take.
        I will not subject be to her disdain:
        The world shall never say I love in vain.

Ibid.

COLLOP

JOHN COLLOP (1625, alive in 1660). By profession a doctor. Author of a book of poems, some loyal stanzas and a prose plea for toleration in religion which achieved a reissue. The poems, *Poesis rediviva*, 1656, are one hundred and twenty-eight in number. They have been badly neglected. Until Mr John Drinkwater drew attention to some of them a few years ago they had been completely ignored. That poet says of "The Leper Cleans'd": "It is a great religious lyric, with a close which is as wonderful as anything in seventeenth-century poetry....It is interesting to note the variation in design midway through the poem, so unexpected and so successful." Collop is in the direct Anglican tradition. He is a skilled metrist and has fierce, spiritual sincerity.

TO THE SOUL

DULL soul aspire,
Thou art not earth, mount higher;
Heav'n gave the spark, to it return the fire!

Let sin ne'er quench
Thy high-flam'd spirit hence;
To earth the heat, to heav'n the flame dispence!

Rejoyce, rejoyce,
Turn, turn, each part a voice;
While to the heart-strings tun'd ye all rejoyce.

The house is swept
Which sin so long foul kept;
The peny's found for which the loser wept.

And purg'd with tears,
God's Image re-appears.
The peny truly shews whose stamp it bears.

⟨ 27 ⟩

Collop

The sheep long lost,
Sin's wilderness oft crost,
Is found, regain'd, return'd; spare, spare no cost!

'Tis heav'ns own suit,
Hark how it woo's you to't;
When Angels needs must speak, shall man be mute?

Poesis rediviva, or Poesie reviv'd, 1656

THE LEPER CLEANS'D

HEAR, Lord, hear,
The Rhet'rick of a tear;
Hear, hear my brest;
While I knock there, Lord take no rest.

Open! ah open wide!
Thou art the door, Lord; open! hide
My sin; a spear once enter'd at thy side.

See! ah, see
A Na'man's leprosie!
Yet here appears
A cleansing Jordan in my tears.

Lord, let the faithless see
Miracles ceas'd, revive in me.
The Leper cleans'd, Blinde heal'd, Dead rais'd by thee.

Whither? ah whither shall I fly?
To heav'n? my sins, ah, sins there cry!
Yet mercy, Lord, O mercy! hear
Th'atoning incense of my prayer.
A broken heart thou'lt not despise.
See! see a Contrite's sacrifice!

Keep, keep, viols of wrath keep still! *Collop*
I'le viols, Lord, of Odors fill:
Of prayers, sighs, grones, and tears a shower;
I'le 'noint, wash, wipe, kisse, wash, wipe, weep;
My tears Lord in thy bottle keep,
Lest flames of lust, and fond desire,
Kindle fresh fuel for thine ire,
Which tears much quench, like Magdalene,
I'le wash thee Lord, till I be clean.

Ibid.

A CHARACTER OF A COMPLEAT GENTLEMAN

To John Cotton Esqr; Heir to the Knowledge and Virtue, as
well as to the Honour and Fortunes Of his Ancestors.
To his Coz. George Boswel Esq; rich in Desert as Fortune.

THOU to the lame art legs, eyes to the blinde,
They their own wants in thy perfections finde;
Thou pluck'st no houses down to rear thy own;
The poor God's houses rear'st out of thy stone:
And not to him who asks bread, givest one.
Thy door is open, and thy heart so too:
Hast both enough, and heart enough to do.
Thou not inclosest to fence out the poor,
But an inclosure art to keep their store.
Sheep eat no men, thy men thy sheep do eat;
In tears of others wil'st not stew thy meat.
To dogs the Children's bread thou dost not give,
Make thy dogs fat, scarce let thy servants live.
Thy father gives thee dirt, thou mak'st it gold;
Virtue refines it to a better mold.
Gold, the Sun's Childe, thou let'st the father see,
That it may make a childe of light of thee.

⟨ 29 ⟩

Collop   Thou bragg'st no stem; think'st vice improves no blood,
Should vice or taint, or virtue speak not good.
For Honour, Conscience dost not put to sale;
Or thy Religion steer by profit's gale.
Imbib'st no dregs ev'n in these lees of time,
A licenc'd ill can'st think no lesser crime.
Thou drink'st no health for to impair thy own,
By th'cup-flush'd face think'st noble blood not shown.
By no rash humour swell'st the Kingdom's spleen,
From whose bulk th'leanness hath of th'body been,
Where he who gains no Idol for his lust,
An Idol Fancy gets of Cits on trust.
While profits th'Prophet that doth teach it there,
Religion shew'd by darker shops like ware.
These not th'world onely, but think God to cheat,
Forge some new light, he's theirs by the deceit.
These take not thee; nor those Hawks tow'ring prize,
While they can grovel in impurities.
Thy Reason is a Hawk, which takes a flight,
As if she'd nest her in a Sphere of light.
What would a nurse more for her childe heav'n woo,
Then to have good, know how to use it too?

                                          Ibid.

ON THE RESURRECTION

ARISE, my God, my Sun arise!
      Arise, thy side
      My sin doth hide;
      Thy blood makes pure,
      Thy wounds me cure,
He ever lives, who with thee dies:
Arise, my God, my Sun, arise.

Abysses on Abysses call;
> Who God denies
> First to him flies;
> Where fiends could dwell,
> And make an hell.
The first sees heav'n of all:
Abysses on Abysses call.

See! ah, see me, purpled o're!
> The scarlet's thine,
> Though the sin were mine:
> Thine was the grave
> My sins would have.
The rising thine, I would implore.
See! ah, see me, purpled o're!

In mercy, Lord, in mercy rise!
> Emit a ray,
> And make a day,
> Where sin's black night
> Hath ravish'd light.
Thou to the blind, Lord, first gav'st eyes;
In mercy, Lord, in mercy rise.

This day we Resurrection call;
> Remove the stone,
> My sins are one:
> Ah! buried in
> The grave of sin;
Shall I no rising have at all?
This day we Resurrection call.

Come, thou Abyss of sweetness, come!
> Come my dear Lord,
> Say but the word

Unto my Soul,
I shall be whole.
Thou for thy self mak'st onely room;
Come, thou Abyss of sweetness, come!

Ibid.

SPIRIT, FLESH

S. Arise, make hast!
F. Whither? ah, whither, flies my soul so fast?
    S. Heav'n calls, obey!
F. 'Tis night; ah stay! 'tis night! thou'lt lose thy way!
    S. The day spring's rose.
F. Ah, but thy sin-black clouds doth interpose!
    S. Those pennance clears;
The Sun succeeds a sacred dew of teares,
    See a full shower!
Heaven suffers voyolence by an holy Power.
    F. Ah heav'n is high!
S. Pray'r lends a Jacob's ladder to the sky.
    Angels descend.
F. Wrestle, ah wrestle! blessing crowns the end.

Ibid.

THE GOOD SAMARITAN

WHY art so sad my soul? ah, why
Doth sorrow make thy bones all dry?
Shall my sin speak so loud, and I not cry?

Thou good Samaritan save!
See, every wound's a grave!
Sins were the Theeves, let me thy mercies have.

See how the priests with them partake!   *Collop*
    And by not pittying new wounds make!
Can pass with hearts unmov'd though their heads shake.

    Nor tears, nor wounds, can pitty win;
    Thy words the twopence; heav'n Lord the Inn.
Thy blood the oyl must cure the wounds of sin.

        Up, up my soul, make hast, arise!
        Yet be not rash, beware, be wise,
        Heav'n loves not a fool's sacrifice!

        The vale's for servants; sin unloose!
        'Tis holy ground; put off thy shoes!
        An Isaack for an off'ring choose!

        Let not an Ismael with him share!
        So up my soul, up, offer there!
        Besiedge, arm'd, enter heav'n by prayer!

        What though thy sins in troops like stars,
        Have menac'd heav'n so oft to wars?
        Heav'n conquering pray'rs atones the jars.

        Rise Sun! stars shall appear no more!
        See, ah, fresh sins like sands of th'shore!
        Pennance lends floods to hide them ore.

                                              Ibid.

COPPINGER

MATTHEW COPPINGER (*fl.* 1682). Probably an actor. Published one volume of verses, *Poems, Songs, and Love-Verses, etc.* 1682.

A SONG

I WILL not tell her that she's fair,
    For that she knows as well as I,
And that her Vertues equal are
    Unto the Glorys of her Eye.

And that I love her well she knows,
    For who can view that Heavenly Face,
Not paying that Respect he owes
    To Beauty bearing such a Grace?

But this I'le tell and tell her true:
    She takes upon her too much State;
For, by the Gods, it would undo
    A King to Love at such a rate!

Let Common Beauties boast the Power
    Of some uncommon Excellence,
And thank Dame Nature for the Dower
    Of that decoying, Charming Sense;

Adorn themselves with Pearls and Gold,
    In Rubies and Rich Diamonds shine,
In choicest Silks that may be sold
    And all to make such Ladies Fine.

These are like some Rich Monument,
    Rais'd all of carv'd and costly Stones,
Painted and Gilt for Ornament;
    But full within of dead Men's Bones.

Such common ways my Clelia scorns,   *Coppinger*
    Her lovely Soul is too sublime;
She's not complete that Cloaths adorns,
    Or does in aught but Nature shine.

Poems, Songs, and Love-Verses, etc. 1682

A LOVER'S COMPLAINT

AH! fainting Breath, there's nought can yield relief
    Unto a wounded Soul, whose murm'ring grief
    Loves no delay, but, like the rising Sun,
Still perseveres until his course is done.
What shall I speak? or what can I devise?
I'le rather dye, than once Apostatize.
Nor shall my panting Breath your shade defame;
I'le honour you, and Idolize your Name;
And though at last you scorn me till I dye,
I needs must love you to Eternity.

Ibid.

TO CLELIA

COY Clelia, veil those Charming Eyes,
    From whose surprise there's none can part;
For he that gazes, surely dies,
    Or leaves behind a conquer'd Heart.

I durst not once presume to look,
    Or cast my wary Eyes aside:
But as a Boy that Cons his Book,
    Close sitting by his Master's side,

⟨ 35 ⟩   3-2

Coppinger

Dares not presume to look awry
　　On Toys that catch the wandering sense;
So if I gaze I surely die:
　　Against those Charms there's no defence.

Thus Heathens, at the Sun's up-rise,
　　Unto the Ground did bow their Head,
Not able with their feeble Eyes
　　To view their God they worshipped.

Ibid.

CUDMORE

DANIEL CUDMORE (1637?–1701). A Devonshire poet who studied at Oxford. Afterwards Rector of Holsworthy, Devon. Author of *Euchodia; a Prayer-Song. Being Sacred Poems, etc.* 1655. He has remained in almost complete obscurity though most of his efforts bear the unmistakable touch of poetry. He is seldom constant to his ability and many of his poems are too long. Full of quaint similes and experimental metres.

From ON SEVERAL OCCASIONS, AND SEVERAL TEXTS OF SCRIPTURE

Mark 7

21. For from within, out of the heart of men, proceed evil thoughts, adulteries, fornications, murthers,
22. Thefts, covetousness, wickedness, deceit, lasciviousness, an evil eye, blasphemy, pride, foolishness.

1

IF could some Delius with divided hands
   Sound the Seas' depth, and on his soul's recorder
   Imprint the wracks, huge rocks, and heaps of sands,
Which there lie scatter'd in confus'd disorder:
     This could he do, by Nature's strength or art,
     Yet none could sound the bottom of the heart.

2

Should some Ship-master make's fore-split the Probe
Of Nature's secrets, and so bring to view
Land to make up a perfect earthly Globe
Which Drake or Kit Columbus never knew:
     Yet, as in the great world, so in his own,
     He must confess there's yet much land unknown.

The heart's a Sea for depth, like Sodom-lake,
Dead, thick, and gross; in it will sink no good:
Th'heart's land's unknown; wherein what monsters make
Their hides and dens, few yet have understood.
> The centre may be purest earth; yet th'heart,
> The bodie's centre's, the corrupter part.

4

Our heart-strings are the cords of vanity;
Their caverns are the devil's lurking-holes;
No fit Triangle for the Trinity;
An habitation more fit for moles:
> Their cauls the veils of damn'd Hypocrisie,
> Thus is sum'd up man's wretched Majestie.

5

If thus the Sun within our firmament
Into a meteor degenerate;
If thus the King within our continent
Let's sin and lust usurp his Royal state:
> If thus corrupted be the bodie's leaven,
> How shall we manchets be prepar'd for heaven?

6

Whe'er Hell be in th'earth's centre, I suspend;
But in man's centre's couch'd an Hell of sin:
Nor do so many lines to th'centre tend,
As in a wicked heart fiends make their Inne:
> Which yet most know no more than can be found
> Where Arethusa windes beneath the ground.

Lord, shew me in the Mirrour of thy Law
The horrour of my heart by bright reflection:
In that thy Glass, there falshood is nor flaw,
Though wickedly some scorn its true direction,
  And whip the Tutor for his discipline;
  Yet Lord direct me by that Glass of thine.

     8

Oh daign my heart with graces to perfume,
And th'rowly purge it from each noisome vapor,
Whose rank infection choaks each neighb'ring room,
And strives to damp my soul's aspiring tapor.
  O make my heart-strings, Lord, thy cords of love;
  So mine according to thy heart shall prove.

        Euchodia; a Prayer-Song, **1655**

ON THE SPRING

MY Sense is ravish'd, when I see
  This happie Season's Jubilee.
  What shall I term it? a new birth,
The resurrection of the earth,
Which hath been buried, we know,
In a cold Winding-sheet of snow.
The Winter's breath had pav'd all o'er
With Crystal Marble th'world's great floor:
But now the earth is livery'd
In verdant suits, by April dy'd;
And, in despight of Boreas' spleen,
Deck'd with a more accomplish'd green.

The gaudy Primrose long since hath
Disclos'd her beauty by each path.
The floods, as freez'd for Chariot-proof,
Were planch'd o'er with a Crystal roof:
Now in their channels sweetly glide,
As Nyle, when they his banks divide.
The trees rob'd of their leafie pride,
With mossie frize had cloath'd each side;
Whose hoary beards seem'd to presage
To blooming youth their winter's age:
But now invite to come and lie
Under their quilted Canopie.
Blithe Damon, like a jolly man,
Long since unto the mountains ran,
Where quietly he sits to pipe,
Whereat his lambs do seem to skip;
Then running to their dams they tug,
With pleasant speed, the swelling dug.
Anon, let's to yon hawthorn steal,
And hearken how sweet Philomele
Grieves not so much at Tereus' crime
As joys to see the Summer's prime.
How to the Spring the whistling Thrush
His Sonnets sings on every bush!
The Sun late squinted from the skye,
And look'd on us with half an eye:
But now with glad and golden chear
Phlegon mounts up our Hemisphere.
Our blood's mild, as if by some art
W'had suck'd some new-born infant's heart.
In brief, quaint Nature seems here nice
In type to shadow Paradice.

Lord, all things bud, and shall I davour   *Cudmore*
Without the sunshine of thy favour?
Wilt never prime? hast passed a doom,
That season never more shall bloom?
Indict not on me such a dearth,
A greater curse then on the earth.
If did my sin in Tereus shape
Act on thy Philomel a rape;
My soul like Progne shall be just,
And on his brats revenge his lust,
Let Primrose-like Repentance rise,
Dew'd by the April of mine eyes:
Then will I not doubt but next thou
Wilt make each grace in order blow.

Ibid.

CUTTS

LORD JOHN CUTTS (1661–1707). Baronet and soldier. His first verses were a rhymed defence of dilettante poets. In 1687 appeared *Poetical Exercises*. He writes a fair, if artificial, love-song.

TO A LADY,

WHO DESIRED ME NOT TO BE
IN LOVE WITH HER

I WILL obey you to my utmost power;
You cannot ask, nor I engage for more.
But if, when I have try'd my utmost Skill,
A Tyde of Love drives back my floating Will,
When on the naked Beach you see me lye,
For Pity's sake you must not let me dye.

Take Pattern by the glorious God of Day,
And raise no Storms but what you mean to lay;
He, when the Charms of his attractive Eye
Have stir'd up Vapours and disturb'd the Sky,
Lets Nature weep and sigh a little while,
And then revives her with a pleasing smile.

If 'tis to try me, use me as you please,
But, when that Tryal's over, give me ease;
Don't torture one that wishes you no harm,
Prepare to cure me, or forbear to Charm.

Poetical Exercises, 1687

A SONG

MADE TO A FRENCH TUNE

ON Racks of Love distended
  Here lies a faithful Swain,
 Wishing his Life were ended,
  Or some Respite to his pain.

The plague of dubious Fate
 Is an Ill beyond enduring,
If I am not worth your curing
 Kill me quickly with your Hate.

But why should Wit and Beauty
 Be guilty of such Crimes?
Sure 'tis a Woman's Duty
 To be merciful sometimes.

With Justice you may slay
 The ungrateful and aspiring,
But the Humble and Admiring
 You should treat a nobler way.

          Ibid.

FAREWELL TO PHILLIS

SET BY MR KING

ONE Look, and I am gone;
 Phillis, my Part is done;
 Death, your pale Rival's come
  And calls me home.

Clasp'd in her frozen Arms
I shall be free from Harms,
And only pity thee
  In misery.

Cutts   For, since your kindness is turn'd into Hate,
From cruel you I'le flye to kinder Fate.

Then, too late,
You'l wish me back again:
Then, too late,
You'l pity him your Eyes have slain.

Ibid.

A SONG

SET BY MR KING

ONLY tell her that I love,
Leave the rest to her and Fate;
Some kind Planet from above
May, perhaps, her pity move;
Lovers on their Stars must wait,
Only tell her that I love.

Why, oh, why should I despair?
Mercy's pictur'd in her Eye;
If she once vouchsafe to hear,
Welcome Hope, and farewel Fear!
She's too good to let me dye:
Why, oh, why should I despair?

Ibid.

DANCER

JOHN DANCER (*fl.* 1660, alive in 1707). Dramatist, connected with Theatre Royal, Dublin. First published in England, 1660. Works consist of several translations from French and Italian, including *Aminta* (from Tasso), 1660; *Nicomede* (from Corneille), 1671; *The Comparison of Plato and Aristotle*, 1673; *Agrippa*, a play of his own, 1675, and some stories. His only poems are found in *Aminta*. They are light, competent lyrics of inconstancy, farewells, resolutions and persuasions to love.

THE VARIETY

THOU sai'st I swore I lov'd thee best,
    And that my heart liv'd in thy breast;
    And now thou wondrest much that I
Should what I swore then, much deny,
And upon this thou taxest me
With faithlessnesse, inconstancy:
      Thou hast no reason so to do,
      Who can't dissemble ne'r must wooe.

That so I lov'd thee 'tis confest,
But 'twas because I judg'd thee best,
For then I thought that thou alone
Wast vertue's, beautie's paragon:
But now that the deceit I find,
To love thee still were to be blind;
      And I must needs confess to thee
      I love in love variety.

Alas! should I love thee alone,
In a short time I should love none;
Who on one well-lov'd feeds, yet,
Once being cloy'd, of all, loaths it;

Dancer   Would'st thou be subject to a fate
            To make me change my love to hate?
                Blame me not then, since 'tis for love
                Of thee, that I inconstant prove.

            And yet in truth 'tis constancy,
            For which I am accus'd by thee;
            To nature those inconstant are,
            Who fix their love on one that's faire;
            Why did she, but for our delight,
            Present such numbers to our sight?
                'Mongst all the earthly kings, there's none
                Contented with one Crown alone.

                                            Aminta, 1660

SHE INCONSTANT

HA! now you think y'have cheated me; oh no!
    I did believe you would do so:
        Who ever did the various wind
    Still constant to one corner find?
    Whenever did the changling air
    Show it self still serene and fair?
Yet we might sooner hope these thus should be,
Than think to find in woman constancy.

We may as well command the Sun not move,
    As you with constancy to love,
        Or bid the sea be free from waves,
        When stormy blustring Boreas raves,
        Nay we as well the Moon might wooe,
        To leave her weekly change as you:
Your nature 'tis, and should you constant be,
I fear you'd prove unnatural to me.

You lighter much than feathers are, and so *Dancer*
    Must move with what e'r wind doth blow,
    Hurried about, now here, now there,
    Now yonder; but yet fixt no where.
    Perhaps at length a gust may be
    To bring you back once more to me;
But Jove forbid: for yet I fear thou'dst move
My ensnar'd soule to ruine in thy love.

                      Ibid.

THE CONQUEST

Gently, kind love restrain, restrain thy hand,
    Keep back thy cruel pricking dart!
    Lest it not wound but kill my heart;
I yeild. Who dare resist if thou command?
    O let it be enough for thee
That thou hast gain'd o'r me the victory;
Do not insult upon my misery!

Shouldst thou continue still to conquer me,
    And shouldst thou not to my o'reflown grief
    Send some small comfort or relief,
Death would at last of both have victory;
    Be merciful and let me live,
Lest while t'inlarge thy power thou dost strive,
Thy cruelty Subjects of life deprive.

I ask no more, but so far pity me
    As with the self same dart
    To wound her frozen heart,
That so she may no more relentlesse be;
    And thus shalt thou two subjects gain,
Who will this victory of thine proclaim,
And ever honour thy all-conquering name.

                      Ibid.

THE FAREWEL

N ow perverse world I'le bid thee quite farewel:
What is there in thee that can please?
Thy greatest joys disturb our ease,
Thy favours thou at too dear rate dost sell.
No, I'll thy slave no longer be,
But quite retreat myself from thee,
Or to some pleasant shade, or to a gloomy Cell.

There in dull silence will I spend my dayes,
Slighting thy favours and my fame;
In vain men seek to get a name,
Or their false glory in thy crouds to raise,
Since that their living trophees must
By time or fate consume to dust,
And then what rests there of their toil-got praise?

Yet in despite of thee my name shall be
The talk of ages yet to come;
In every time there shall be some,
Which shall applaud me more for leaving thee,
Then those fond simple fools who do
Imbrace thy woes and honours too,
And make me famous to posterity.

Ibid.

THE RESOLUTION

N ow by that beauty I so much adore,
I am resolv'd to dote no more,
No longer shall my passions strive
Me of my reason to deprive,
No longer will I subject be,
But nobly set my heart at liberty.

Then go dear heart, and be no more confin'd   *Dancer*
    To a woman's changling mind.
    Why should'st thou a subject be
    To their self-will'd tyranny?
    Break, break thy bands and fetters; know,
Subject to her, thou'rt subject to a foe.

There's nought in her that thee her slave hath made;
    'Tis thou that hast thy selfe betraid,
    By fanc'ing that her beauties shine
    Like something more then halfe divine:
    Think then thy selfe deceiv'd to be,
Thou'rt undeceiv'd, and art than thought more free.

'Tis men alone that womens' Empire raise,
    By wooing them with fanci'd praise;
    When, if we would their masters be,
    They must grant Superiority:
    Nay, did we cease to flatter thus,
'Twould not be long ere they would flatter us.

Cease then, my heart, and dote no more in vain,
    Thou never thus the fort wilt gain;
    No more upon entreaties stand,
    But learn like her how to command;
    Those Castles which find no remorse,
On summons must be taken in by force.

                          Ibid.

DANIEL

GEORGE DANIEL (1616–1657). His verses were left in MS.
They were edited in 1878 by A. B. Grosart. A number are
worthy of rescue from the oblivion into which they have,
for a second time, sunk.

THE SPRING

Now the Springe enters; now the Sun doth cheare
The quickn'd Earth; and trees by Cold made bare
Now gin to bud; the Earth doth now begin
To flourish in her Sweet and glorious Trimme;
The Silver Streams bound up by Winter's Cold
Glide fairly, where they murmured of old;
The goodly meadowes, russet late, and dead,
In a fresh Dresse are now apparelled;
The mountaine tops are bar'd, and where the Snow
Late covered, the Spring begins to Show.
Thither, the Lads, dull'd with the Winter's rest,
To joy in wonted Sports doe gladly hast;
Now Joyes the Industrious Bee, and the Ant now,
(Emblems of Providence), her selfe doth Show, /
Warme in her Winter's Store; doth now againe
Labour, and make provision to sustaine
Her little bodie for the after-day;
Now flyes the maggot, in her paintings gay,
(Signe of fair weather), and doth now invite
Decrepit years to tast the Spring's delight.
I will not call the cuckooe with the Spring;
(Unnatural, foolish bird), let her voyce ringe
T'affright the Citie, and an Omen carrie
Of fate, to fooles and old men, when they marrie.

But here the Redbrest and gray Linnets Singe,   *Daniel*
The poore wren flutters with an Eager wing,
To gaine yond' highest Sprig, and there doth pay
A Ceremonious Himme to welcome day;
Whilst from that Grove, the haples Philomel
Sweetly, though sadly, doth her Story tell;
The little Dazies shake their Deawie locks,
The ambitious Woodbine climbs againe, and mocks
The tardie Gilliflower; the Lillye in
Her liveing Robe of Innocence doth Shine;
For those of Cost and Art to me are poor:
Nature is Rich and Curious in her Store;
And this same Marigold, or Violet here,
To the transplanted Tulip, I prefere;
Loe, where the Larke, borne on her active wing,
Pouers forth her Song of Joy unto the Spring;
Lambs joyous friske, and play now each with other,
Neglect the Teate, and leave the Ewe, their mother;
Inspired with the Time, may my Muse frame
Notes with the Larke, be Sportive with the Lambe.

The Poems of George Daniel (ed. 1878)

ODE 1

WHEN I am gone, and these of mine remaine,
        If these, or ought which I call mine, shall
                stay;
Read over what I leave, and you againe
Adde to the sand of Time; and give my Day
    As glorious Life as when I stood to breath:
    Hee dyes not, who Survives his Dust in Death.

⟨ 51 ⟩   4-2

Daniel   I doe not Beg a Life beyond my Fate,
       Or ask the Courtesie you would not give;
'Tis neither you nor I can set a Date
To written Numbers, if a Muse bid live;
      And these may live; who knowes, when winds disperse
      My Earth in Atomes, Men shall read this verse?

                                             Ibid.

ONE DESIRING ME TO READ, BUT SLEPT IT OUT; WAKENING

NAY doe not Smile: my Lips shall rather dwell
       For ever on my Pipe,
   Then read to you one word or Sillable.
       You are not ripe
     To Iudge, or Apprehend
     Of Witt. I'le rather Spend
Six howers together in Tobacco-taking,
Then read to you, and cannot keep you wakeing.

                                             Ibid.

DUFFETT

THOMAS DUFFETT (*fl.* 1678). Milliner, then playwright and poet. His only book of verses was *New Poems, Songs, Prologues and Epilogues, set by the most eminent Musicians about the Town,* 1676.

UNCERTAIN LOVE

THE lab'ring man that Plants or Sows,
His certain times of Profit knows.
Seamen the roughest tempest scorn,
Hoping at last a rich return.
But my too much-lov'd Celia's mind
Is more inconstant and unkind
Than stormy weather, Sea or Wind.

Now with assured Hope rais'd high,
I think no man so blest as I;
Hope, that a dying Saint may own,
To see and hear her speak alone.
What if I snatch one kiss or more?
Where Heaven gives a wealthy store,
'Tis to be bounteous to the poor.

But e'r my swiftest thought can thence
Convey a blessing to my sense,
My hope like Fairy treasure's gone,
Although I never made it known.
From all untruth my heart is clean,
No other Love can enter in,
Yet Celia's ne'r will come agen.

*New Poems, Songs, Prologues
and Epilogues,* 1676

TO FRANCELIA

Iɴ cruelty you greater are,
    Then those fierce Tyrants who decreed,
The Noblest prisoner ta'n in war,
    Should to their gods a Victim bleed.

A year of pleasures and delight,
    The happy prisoner there obtain'd,
And three whole daies e'r death's long night,
    In pow'r unlimited he reign'd.

To your Victorious Eyes I gave
    My heart a willing Sacrifice;
A tedious year have been your slave;
    Felt all the pains Hate could devise.

But two short hours of troubl'd Bliss,
    For all my suffrings you restore;
And wretched I must die for this,
    And never never meet you more.

Never, how dismally it sounds!
    If I must feel eternal pain,
Close up a while my bleeding wounds,
    And let me have my three daies' reign.

Ibid.

ON A ROSE TAKEN FROM FRANCELIA'S BREAST

Pᴏᴏʀ hapless emblem of Amyntor's heart,
    Thy blooming beauty's overcast;
Deep shades of grief seem to o'erspread each part,
    Yet still thy fragrant sweets do last.

Thou wert not, when my dearest nymph is kind,   *Duffett*
    In all thy pride so blest as I,
She gone, my wounded heart thy fate does find,
    So does it droop, and so will die.

What joyful blushes did thy leaves adorn,
    How gay, how proudly didst thou swell,
When in Francelia's charming bosom worn,
    That Paradise where Gods would dwell.

Oh had my heart thy happy place possest,
    It never had from thence been torn,
But like a Phoenix in her spicy nest,
    It still should live and ever burn.

No wonder thy perfume so near thy death
    Still lasts, though thy vermilion's gone:
Thy sweets were borrowed from her sweeter breath,
    Thy fading colour was thy own.

See how my burning sighs thy leaves have dried,
    Where I have suck'd the stolen sweets:
So does the amorous youth caress his bride,
    And print hot kisses in her lips.

Hadst thou ungathered fall'n among the rest
    Lost and forgotten thou hadst been,
Thou had'st not flourished in Francelia's breast
    Nor been the subject of my pen.

Amber dissolved and beaten spices smell,
    That gold is valued most that's proved;
Coy beauty's lost, but lasting fame will tell
    Their praise that love and are beloved.

                                                        Ibid.

LIBERTY, Liberty!
Reason and Love are at war,
No more on wild Passion I'll wait,
Or cringe to an upstart Despair,
The creature of idle conceit:
Draw up, my thoughts, let Shame the fight begin,
Charge to the heart, oh let not Hope get in;
'Tis Love's hero; if that appear in his defence,
A thousand thousand reasons cannot force him thence.

Victory, Victory!
Love the usurper is fled,
His flames and his arrows are spent,
The toys by which fools are misled
To adore what themselves do invent.
The thing appears that did support his cause,
How pale she looks that to my heart gave laws!
The Nymph's vanish'd, set are the suns that made me blind,
And only woman, vain, weak woman's left behind.

Phillida, Phillida!
What's of my Goddess become?
Oh where is the shape and the mien,
Whose presence has oft struck me dumb,
Whose beauty I thought all divine?
As in the dark to one o'ercome by fear
Deformed shapes and sprites seem to appear,
The fond lover strange wonders in his nymph does find,
When all the charms are in his own deluded mind.

Ibid.

ELYS

EDMUND ELYS (1635, alive in 1707). Anglican minister of East Allington in Devonshire. Author of numerous sermons, meditations, translations and pamphlets. He published four volumes of sorry verses, *Dia Poemata*, 1655; *An Alphabet of Elegiack Groans*, 1656; *Divine Poems*, 1658; *Epigrammata*, 1668. There is an occasional poem of merit.

MELANCHOLY

'TIS Pia Mater in Discolour'd Weeds:
    A Checker'd Plat-form of Phantastic Deeds:
    The Brain-Filme wrought into a Dismall Shroud:
The Sun o' th' Little World in a thick Cloud:
Swift Thought turn'd Fairy: Wild wit gone astray:
A Fancy, that i' th' Dark hath lost its Way.

Dia Poemata, 1655

TO MRS A. S. ON THE DEATH OF HER TWO FIRST CHILDREN

YOUR Fair Cheeks with Tears sprinkl'd shew
    Like Roses Pearled o're with Dew.
    But be not so Discomforted:
Your Babes Departed are not Dead.
To keep them from all casuall Harmes,
Their Saviour takes them in His Armes.
These Olive-Branches, by his care,
In Paradise Transplanted are.
So they become, by their Decease,
A Garland to the Prince of Peace.

Ibid.

⟨ 57 ⟩

"That which I doe, I allow not: for what I would, that
doe I not; but what I hate, that do I." Rom. 7. 15.

1

MY Mind keeps out the Host of Sin;
  Sense lets 'em in:
I'th Phantasie, as i' th' Trojan Horse,
  They Hide their Force.
Till opportunity they find
To Sally, and subdue the Mind.

2

My Childish Soule oft Cries for what
  It straight doth Hate.
My Lusts, whom Reason should Controle,
  War 'gainst my Soule;
And having got the Victory,
Bring me into Captivity.

3

My Love against My will is hurl'd
  Upon the World:
I See not in the Darke. I know
  Not what I Doe
When Sin besets me; so befool'd,
I hate to do even what I would.

4

O, when shall my lost Soule obtaine
  Her Selfe againe?
To Act Her owne Hate, and Desire?
  O Sacred Fire!
Refine my Heart; and that it be
Kept Pure, O Lord, I give it Thee.

Divine Poems, 1658

"EPHELIA"

"EPHELIA" (*fl.* 1679). The identity of this Restoration
poetess remains unknown. There is no evidence for associating
her with a "Joan Phillips" who may have been a relative of
Katharine Phillips, "the Matchless Orinda". Her verses
reveal a strong personality. They are essentially Restoration
in feeling and style, yet her frank utterance and virile
intensity often look back to Donne. There is courage and
lack of sentimentality. Her book *Female Poems on Several
Occasions* was issued in 1679, and again "with large additions" in 1682. Two songs from Dryden's plays are included
in her volume, one of which Dryden may well have borrowed
from her.

UPON HIS LEAVING HIS MISTRESS

'TIS not that I am weary grown
  Of being yours, and yours alone:
  But with what face can I incline
To damn you to be onely mine?
You whom some tender Power did fashion
By Merit and by Inclination,
The joy at least of one whole Nation?

Let meaner Spirits of your Sex
With humbler aims their thoughts perplex;
And boast, if by their Arts they can
Contrive to wake one happy Man:
Whilst mov'd by an impartial sence,
Favours like Nature you dispence
With universal Influence.

See the kind seed-receiving Earth
To every grain affords a birth:

On her no Showers unwelcome fall,
Her Willing Womb retains them all.
And shall my Celia be confin'd?
No, live up to thy mighty mind,
And be the Mistress of Mankind.

Female Poems on Several Occasions, 1679

TO PHYLOCLES, INVITING HIM TO FRIENDSHIP

Best of thy Sex! if Sacred Friendship can
Dwell in the Bosom of inconstant Man,
As cold and clear as Ice, as Snow unstain'd,
With Love's loose Crimes unsully'd, unprofan'd:

Or you a Woman with that Name dare trust,
And think to Friendship's Ties we can be just:
In a strict League together we'l combine,
And let our Friendship's bright example shine.

We will forget the Difference of Sex,
Nor shall the World's rude Censure us Perplex.
Think Me all Man: my Soul is Masculine,
And Capable of as great Things as Thine.

I can be Gen'rous, Just and Brave,
Secret and Silent as the Grave,
And if I cannot yield Relief,
I'le Sympathize in all thy Grief.

I will not have a Thought from thee I'le hide,
In all my Actions Thou shalt be my Guide;
In every Joy of mine Thou shalt have share,
And I will bear a part in all thy Care.

Why do I vainly Talk of what we'l do?
We'l mix our Souls, you shall be Me, I You;
And both so one it shall be hard to say
Which is Phylocles, which Ephelia.

Our Ties shall be as strong as the Chains of Fate,
Conqu'rors and Kings our Joys shall Emulate;
Forgotten Friendship, held at first Divine,
T'its native Purity we will refine.

Ibid.

FIRST FAREWEL TO J. G.

FAREWEL my dearer half, joy of my heart,
Heaven only knows how loth I am to part:
Whole Months but hours seem, when you are here,
When absent, every Minute is a Year:
Might I but always see thy charming Face,
I'de live on Racks, and wish no easier place.
But we must part, your Interest says we must;
Fate, me no longer with such Treasure trust.
I wou'd not tax you with Inconstancy,
Yet Strephon, you are not so kind as I:
No Interest, no nor Fate it self has pow'r
To tempt me from the Idol I adore:
But since you needs must go, may Africk be
Kinder to you than Europe is to me:
May all you meet and every thing you view
Give you such transport as I met in you.
May no sad thoughts disturb your quiet mind,
Except you'l think of her you left behind.

Ibid.

WHAT Miracles this childish God has wrought!
Things strange above belief! Who wou'd
have thought
My Temper could be to this Tameness brought?

I, who the wanton Boy so long defi'd,
And his Fantastick Godhead did deride,
And laugh'd at Lovers with insulting Pride,

Now pale and faint beneath his Altar lie,
Own him a great and glorious Deity,
And want the pitty that I did deny.

For my proud Victor does my Tears neglect,
Smiles at my Sighs, treats me with disrespect:
And if I do complain, with frowns I'm check't.

Though all I sue for be the empty bliss
Of a kind look, or at the most a kiss;
Yet he's so cruel to deny me this.

Before my Passion struck my Reason blind,
Such Generosity dwelt in my mind,
I car'd for none, and yet to all was kind.

But now I tamely bend, and sue in vain
To one that takes delight t'increase my pain
And proudly does Me and my Love disdain.

Ibid.

WHY do I love? go, ask the Glorious Sun
        Why every day it round the world doth run:
        Ask Thames and Tyber, why they Ebb and Flow:
Ask Damask Roses, why in June they blow:
Ask Ice and Hail the reason why they're cold:
Decaying Beauties, why they will grow Old.
They'l tell thee Fate, that every thing doth move,
Inforces them to this, and me to Love.
There is no Reason for our Love or Hate,
'Tis irresistable as Death or Fate:
'Tis not his face; I've sence enough to see
That is not good, though doated on by me:
Nor is't his Tongue that has this Conquest won,
For that at least is equall'd by my own:
His Carriage can to none obliging be,
'Tis Rude, Affected, full of Vanity:
Strangely Ill-natur'd, Peevish, and Unkind,
Unconstant, False, to Jealousie inclin'd;
His Temper cou'd not have so great a Pow'r,
'Tis mutable, and changes every hour:
Those vigorous Years that Women so Adore,
Are past in him; he's twice my Age and more;
And yet I love this false, this worthless Man,
With all the Passion that a Woman can
Doat on his Imperfections; though I spy
Nothing to Love, I love, and know not why.
Sure 'tis Decreed in the dark Book of Fate,
That I shou'd Love, and he shou'd be ingrate.

Ibid.

STREPHON I saw, and started at the sight,
　And interchangeably looked red and white;
　I felt my Blood run swiftly to my heart
And a chill Trembling seize each outward part;
My Breath grew short, my Pulse did quicker beat,
My Heart did heave as it wou'd change its Seat;
A faint, cold Sweat o're all my Body spread,
A gidy Megrim wheel'd about my head.
When for the reason of this change I sought,
I found my Eyes had all the mischief wrought,
For they my Soul to Strephon had betray'd,
And my weak heart his willing Victim made;
The Traytors conscious of the Treason
They had committed 'gainst my Reason,
Look'd down with such a bashful, guilty Fear,
As made their Fault to every Eye appear.
Though the first fatal Look too much had done,
The lawless wanderers wou'd still gaze on,
Kind Looks repeat and Glances steal, till they
Had look'd my Liberty and Heart away.
Great Love, I yield; send no more Darts in vain,
I am already fond of my soft Chain;
Proud of my Fetters, so pleas'd with my state
That I the very Thought of Freedom hate.
O Mighty Love! thy Art and Pow'r joyn,
To make his Frozen breast as warm as mine;
But if thou try'st and can'st not make him kind,
In Love such pleasant, real Sweets I find,
That, though attended with Despair it be,
'Tis better still than a wild Liberty.

Ibid.

SONG

"Ephelia"

Y ou wrong me, Strephon, when you say
    I'me Jealous or Severe,
    Did I not see you Kiss and Play
        With all you came a-neer?
Say, did I ever Chide for this,
    Or cast one Jealous Eye
On the bold Nymphs that snatch'd my Bliss
    While I stood wishing by?

Yet though I never disapprov'd
    This modish Liberty,
I thought in them you only lov'd
    Change and Variety:
I vainly thought my Charms so strong,
    And you so much my Slave,
No Nymph had Pow'r to do me Wrong,
    Or break the Chains I gave.

But when you seriously Address
    With all your winning Charms
Unto a Servile Shepherdess,
    I'le throw you from my Arms:
I'de rather chuse you should make Love
    To every Face you see,
Than Mopsa's dull Admirer prove
    And let Her Rival me.

Ibid.

Know, Celadon, in vain you use
    These little Arts to me:
Though Strephon did my Heart refuse
    I cannot give it thee;
His harsh Refusal hath not brought
    Its Value yet so low,
That what was worth that Shepherd's Thoughts
    I shou'd on You bestow.

Nor can I love my Strephon less
    For his ungrateful Pride,
Though Honour does, I must confess
    My guilty Passion chide:
That lovely Youth I still adore,
    Though now it be in vain;
But yet of him I ask no more
    Than Pity for my Pain.

Ibid.

FANE

MILDMAY FANE (1602–1665). The second Earl of West-
morland, who was a Royalist soldier and afterwards Lord-
Lieutenant of Northamptonshire. A friend of Herrick, Cleve-
land, etc. Author of a curious book of verses, mostly religious,
entitled *Otia Sacra*, 1648. It is embellished with mystical emblems and folding leaves, and takes the reader to Dryden's
"peaceful province in acrostic land" where one poor word
is tortured ten-thousand ways. But Fane often rises to a much
higher level.

A DEDICATION OF MY FIRST SON

I s it not fit the Mould and Frame
    Of man, should dedicate the same
    To God, who first Created it; and t'give
To Him the first fruit of that Span we live?

In the world's Infancy could Hannah tell,
Shee ought to Offer her sonn Samuel
    To Him that made him, and refine
    That Sacrifice with Flowre and Wine?

    Was Abram's long expected seed
    From Sarah's womb condemn'd to bleed?
And shall the time now they grow Old, conclude
In faithlessness, and in ingratitude?

Let shame awake us, and where blessings fall,
Let every one become a Prodigall
    In paying vows of thanks, and bring
    The first, and best for Offering.

Where am I then, whom God hath deign'd to bless
With hopes of a succeeding hapiness
    Unto my house? Why is't I stand
    At th'Altar with an Empty hand?

Fane

Have I no Herds, no Flocks, no Oyl,
No Incense-bearing-Shebah-foyl?
Is not my Grainary stor'd with Flowre that's fine?
Are not my Strutted Vessels full of Wine?

What Temporall Blessing's wanting to suffice
And furnish out a lively Sacrifice,
    Save onely this, to make a Free-
    Will-offering of an Infancy?

    Which if I should not doe, that pil'd-
    Up wood, whereon lay Sarah's childe;
The Temple would accuse me, where the son
Of Elk'na first had Dedication.

    Wherefore accept, I pray thee, this
    Thou'st given, and my first Sonn is:
Let him be Thine, and from his Cradleling,
Begin his services first reckoning.

Grant, with his Dayes, thy Grace increase, and fill
His Heart, nor leave there room to harbour ill;
    That in the Progress of His years
    He may express whose badg He wears.

Otia Sacra, 1648

IN OBITUM BEN. JOHNS. POETAE EXIMII

HE who began from Brick and Lime
    The Muses' Hill to climbe;
    And whilom busied in laying Ston,
Thirsted to drink of Helicon;
Changing his Trowell for a Pen,
Wrote straight the Temper not of Dirt but Men.

⟨ 68 ⟩

Now sithence that He is turn'd to Clay, and gon,   *Fane*
      Let those remain of th'occupation
He honor'd once, square Him a Tomb, and say
His craft exceeded farr a Dawber's way.
      Then write upon't He could no longer tarry,
      But was return'd again unto the quarry.   *Ibid.*

OCCASION'D BY SEEING A WALK OF BAY TREES

No Thunder blasts Jove's Plant, nor can
      Misfortune warp an honest Man;
      Shaken He may be, by some one
Or other Gust, Unleav'd by none:
Though tribulation's sharp and keen,
His Resolutions keep Green;
And whilst Integrity's his wall,
His Year's all Spring, and hath no Fall.   *Ibid.*

IN PRAISE OF FIDELIA

Get thee a Ship well-rigg'd and tight,
      With Ordnance store, and Man'd for fight,
      Snug in Her Timbers' Mould for th' Seas,
Yet large in Hould for Merchandies;
Spread forth her Cloth, and Anchors waigh,
And let her on the Curl'd-waves play,
Till, Fortune-tow'd, she chance to meet
Th'Hesperian home-bound Western Fleet;
Then let her board 'um, and for Price
Take Gold-ore, Sugar-canes, and Spice;—
      Yet when all these Sh'hath brought ashore,
      In my Fidelia I'le finde more.   *Ibid.*

⟨ 69 ⟩

VIRTUS VERA NOBILITAS

W HAT doth He get who ere prefers
The Scutchions of His Ancesters?
This Chimney-piece of Gold or Brass,
That Coat of Armes Blazon'd in glass;
When those with time and age have end,
Thy Prowess must thyself commend.
The smooty shadows of some one
Or other's Trophies, carv'd in stone,
Defac'd, are things to whet, not try
Thine own Heroicism by.
For cast how much thy Merits's score
Fall short of those went thee before;
By so much art thou in arrear
And stain'st Gentility, I fear.
True nobleness doth those alone engage
Who can add Vertues to their Parentage.

Ibid.

MY HAPPY LIFE

TO A FRIEND

D EAREST in Friendship, if you'll know
Where I my self, and how, bestow,
Especially when as I range,
Guided by Nature, to love change,
Beleeve, it is not to advance
Or add to my inheritance;
Seeking t'engross by Power amiss
What any other Man calls his:
But full contented with my owne,
I let all other things alone;

⟨ 70 ⟩

Which better t'enjoy without strife,   *Fane*
I settle to a Countrey life.
And in a sweet retirement there
Cherish all Hopes, but banish fear,
Offending none; so for defence
Arm'd Capapee with Innocence,
I do dispose of my time thus,
To make it more propitious.
    First, my God serv'd, I doe commend
The rest to some choice Book or Friend,
Wherein I may such Treasure finde
T'inrich my nobler part, the Minde.
And that my Body Health comprise,
Use too some moderate Exercise;
Whether invited to the field
To see what Pastime that can yield,
With horse, or hound, or hawk, or t'bee
More taken with a well-grown Tree;
Under whose Shades I may reherse
The holy Layes of Sacred Verse;
Whilst in the Branches pearched higher,
The wing'd Crew sit as in a quier:
This seems to me a better noise
Than Organs, or the dear-bought voice
From Pleaders breath in Court and Hall
At any time is stockt withall:
For here one may, (if marking well),
Observe the Plaintive Philomel
Bemoan her sorrows, and the Thrush
Plead safety through Defendant Bush;
The Popingay in various die
Performes the Sergeant, and the Pie
Chatters, as if she would revive

The Old Levite prerogative,
And bring new Rotchets in again;
Till Crowes and Jackdaws in disdain
Of her Pide-feathers chase her thence,
To yeeld to their preheminence.
For you must know't observ'd of late,
That Reformation in the State
Begets no less by imitation
Amidst this chirping feather'd Nation;
Cuckoes Ingrate and Woodcocks some
Here are, which cause they't seasons come,
May be compar'd to such as stand
At Terms, and their returns command.
And, lest Authority take cold,
Here's th'Ivye's guest of wonder, th'Owl,
Rufft like a Judge, and with a Beak,
As it would give the charge and speak:
Then 'tis the Goose and Buzzards art
Alone, t'perform the Clients part;
For neither Dove nor Pigeon shall,
Whilst they are both exempt from gall.
The Augur Hern, and soaring Kite,
Kalendar weather in their flight,
As doe the Cleanlier Ducks, when they
Dive voluntary, wash, prune, play,
With the fair Cygnet, whose delight
Is to out-vie the snow in white.
And therefore alwayes seeks to hide
Her feet, lest they allay her pride.
The Moor-hen, Dobchick, Water-rail,
With little Washdish or Wagtail;
The Finch, the Sparrow, Jenny Wren,
With Robin that's so kinde to men;

The Whitetail and Tom Tit obey   *Fane*
Their seasons, bill and tread, then lay;
The Lyrick Lark doth early rise,
And, mounting, payes her sacrifice;
Whilst from some hedg, or close of furrs,
The Partridge calls its Mate, and churrs;
And that the Countrey seem more pleasant,
Each heath hath Powt, and wood yeelds Phesant;
Junoe's delight, with Cock and Hens,
Turkies, are my Domestick friends;
Nor doe I bird of Prey inlist,
But what I carry on my Fist;
Now not to want a Court, a King-
Fisher is here with Purple wing,
Who brings me to the spring-head, where
Crystall is Lymbeckt all the yeere,
And every Drop distil'd, implies
An Ocean of Felicities;
Whilst calculating, it spins on,
And turns the Pebbles one by one,
Administering to eye and eare
New Stars, and musick like the Sphere;
When every Purle Calcin'd doth run,
And represent such from the Sun.
    Devouring Pike here hath no place,
Nor is it stor'd with Roach or Dace;
The Chub or Cheven not appeare,
Nor Miller's Thumbs, nor Gudgeons here,
But nobler Trowts, beset with stones
Of Rubie and of Diamonds,
Bear greatest sway; yet some intrench,
As sharp-finn'd Pearch, and healing Tench;
The stream's too pure for Carp to lie,

Fane   Subject to perspicuitie;
For it must here be understood
There are no beds of sand and Mud,
But such a Gravell as might pose
The best of Scholars to disclose,
And books and learning all confute,
Being clad in water Tissue sute.
These cool delights help'd with the air
Fann'd from the Branches of the fair
Old Beech, or Oak, enchantments tie
To every sense's facultie;
And master all those powers should give
The will any prerogative:
Yet when the Scorching Noon-dayes heat
Incommodates the Lowing Neat
Or Bleating flock, hither each one
Hasts to be my Companion.
And when the Western Skie with red
Roses bestrews the Day-star's bed,
The wholesome Maid comes out to Milk
In russet-coats, but skin like Silk;
Which, though the Sun and Air dies brown,
Will yeeld to none of all the Town
For softness, and her breath's sweet smell
Doth all the new-milcht Kie excell:
She knows no rotten teeth, nor hair
Bought, or Complexion t'make her fair,
But is her own fair wind and dress,
Not envying Citie's happiness:
Yet as she would extend some pitty
To the drain'd Neat, she frames a ditty
Which doth inchant the beast, untill
It patiently lets her Paile fill;

This doth the babbling Eccho catch   *Fane*
And so at length to me't doth reach.
Straight roused up, I verdict pass,
Concluding from this bonny Lass
And the Birds' strains, 'tis hard to say
Which taught Notes first, or she, or they.
Thus ravish'd, as the night draws on
Its sable Curtain, in I'm gon
To my poor Cell, which 'cause 'tis mine,
I judge it doth all else out-shine:
Hung with content and weather-proof,
Though neither Pavement nor roof
Borrow from Marble-quarr below,
Or from those Hills where Cedars grow.
There I embrace and kiss my Spouse,
Who, like the Vesta to the house,
A Sullibub prepares to show
By care and love what I must owe.
   Then calling in the Spawn and frie,
Who whilst they live ne'er let us die,
But every face is hers or mine,
Though minted yet in lesser Coin,
She takes an Apple, I a Plumbe,
Encouragements for all and some,
Till in return they crown the herth
With innocent and harmless merth,
Which sends us Joyfull to our rest,
More than a thousand others blest.

Ibid.

⟨ 75 ⟩

A HAPPY LIFE

THAT which Creates a happy life
Is substance left, not gain'd by strife,
A fertile and a Thankfull mold,
A Chimney alwayes free from Cold;
Never to be the Client, or
But seldome times the Counsellor.
A Minde content with what is fit,
Whose strength doth most consist in Wit;
A Body nothing prone to be
Sick, a Prudent Simplicitie;
Such Friends as of one's own rank are;
Homely fare, not sought from farre;
The table without Arts help spread;
A night in Wine not buried,
Yet drowning Cares; a Bed that's blest
With true Joy, Chastity, and rest;
Such short, sweet Slumber as may give
Less time to die in't, more to live:
  Thine own Estate whate're commend,
  And wish not for, nor fear thine end.

Ibid.

TO RETIREDNESS

NEXT unto God, to whom I owe
What e're I here enjoy below,
I must indebted stand to Thee,
Great Patron of my Libertie;
For in the Cluster of affaires,
Whence there are dealing severall shares,

As in a Trick Thou hast conveigh'd   *Fane*
Into my hand what can be said;
Whilst he who doth himself possess,
Makes all things pass him seem farr less.

Riches and Honors that appear
Rewards to the Adventurer,
On Either tide of Court or Seas
Are not attain'd nor held with ease,
But as unconstancy bears sway,
Quickly will fleet and Ebb away:
And oft when Fortune those Confers,
She gives them but for Torturers;
When with a Minde Ambition-free,
These, and much more, come home to Me.

Here I can sit, and sitting under
Some portions of His works of wonder,
Whose all are such, observe by reason
Why every Plant obeys its season;
How the Sap rises, and the Fall
Wherein They shake off Leaves and all:
Then how again They bud and spring,
Are laden for an Offering:
Which whilst my Contemplation sees,
I am taught Thankfulness from trees.

Then turning over Nature's leaf,
I mark the Glory of the Sheaf,
For every Field's a severall page
Desciphering the Golden Age;
So that without a Miner's pains,
Or Indie's reach, here plenty raigns;

Fane

Which, watred from above, implies,
That our acknowledgments should rise
To Him that thus creates a birth
Of Mercies for us out of Earth.

Here is no other Case in Law
But what the Sun-burnt Hat of Straw
With crooked Sickle reaps and bindes—
Up into Sheaves to help the hindes;
Whose arguing alon's in this,
Which Cop lies well, and which amiss,
How the Hock-Cart with all its gear
Should be trick'd up, and what good cheer
Bacon with Cook's reports express,
And how to make the Tenth goe less.

There are no other Warrs or Strife's—
Encouragers, shrill Trumpets, Fyfes,
Or horrid Drumms, but what Excels
All Musick, Nature's Minstrels
Piping and Chirping, as they sit
Embowr'd in branches, dance to it;
And, if at all Those doe contest,
It is in this, but which sings best;
And when they have contended long,
I, though unseen, must judge the Song.

Thus out of fears or noise of Warr,
Crowds and the clamourings at Barr,
The Merchant's dread, th'unconstant tides,
With all Vexations besides,
I hugg my Quiet, and alone
Take thee for my Companion,

And deem in doing so, I've all   *Fane*
I can True Conversation call;
For so my Thoughts by this retreat
Grow stronger, like contracted heat.

Whether on Nature's Book I muse,
Or else some other writes on't use
To spend the time in, every line
Is not excentrick but Divine;
And, though all others downward tend,
These look to heaven and ascend
From whence they came; where, pointed high,
They ravish into Mysterie,
To see the footsteps here are trod
Of mercy by a Gracious God.
                                              Ibid.

FARLEY

ROBERT FARLEY (*fl.* 1639). A Scotsman at the court of
James I. Author of two volumes of verses, *Kalendarium
Humanae Vitae, The Kalendar of Man's Life,* 1638, and
Lychnocausia...Lights, Morall Emblems, etc. 1638. The prin-
cipal poems of the former are in English and Latin, and are
decorated with amusing, and sometimes charming, woodcuts.
Most of Farley's work is mild and pleasant.

APRILL, OR MAN'S INFANCIE

THINE Infant, (Lord), to be I crave,
    Let not my gray haires sinne to grave.
    My Soule doth cry; still thou it Lord
With milke of thy eternall Word.
Author of Grace, nurse Grace in me,
So I at length shall strengthen'd be.
Clense me from first and second guilt,
Onely thou canst (Lord) if thou wilt;
Then shall I be a Dennizon
There, where uncleannesse commeth none.
Let not Hell's Siren lull asleepe
My soule to drowne it in the deepe;
Lord make it watch for Heav'ns joyes,
Regarding nothing worldly toyes.
Behold my soule, rock't too and fro,
Doth cry for feare and cannot goe;
Now least in storme it drowned be,
Take it into the ship with Thee.
So shall Thou thinke me to be thine,
And I shall thinke thy kingdome mine;
So shall my soule thy mercies prove
And learne thy mercies how to love.

Kalendarium Humanae Vitae, 1638

⟨ 80 ⟩

OCTOBER, OR MIDDLE AGE   *Farley*

Our lot is elsewhere, joy shall come at last,
Then gladly shall we thinke of troubles past.

From morning's East, unto the evening's West,
From South to North, as Poles doe rise and fall,
Men framing Fortune still seeke for the best,
And oft too curious are deceiv'd of all.
They seeke what fire and water can destroy,
Or moth consume, or these can steale away,
Or wherin they doe pave their greatest joy,
The enemy can take it as a prey.
Heav'n hath my treasure with my Lord and King,
With companies of glorious Saints in blisse,
Where holie quires doe dance, triumph and sing,
They follow, and our Saviour leader is.
Here Nectar rivers every where doe flow,
Joy without sorrow, holy daliance,
Here stands Ambrosia's heapes, whereere you goe,
And what immortall glory can advance.
If you should multiply ten thousand ages,
They shall not end this joy and glorious light,
Nay, though you go beyond ten thousand stages,
Nor all the dayes which never shall know night.
Hither lead me, O Lord, through all distresse,
O're mountains of the land, rockes of the seas,
Through whatsoever hath no quietnesse,
Through stormes and thunder, if it so Thee please.
So that the Haven of this my voyage be
Heav'ns rest; so that the goale be of my race,
The Court of Angels, who attend on Thee,
And in thy Father's house some dwelling place.

Ibid.

A THOUSAND evils this my life doth spend,
　　At length fierce Boreas thereto puts an end:
　　My light, my heat, my flame and all is past;
Onely, whilst breath remaines, my hope doth last.
This life of ours is tost to and againe,
Time and unconstant Fortune workes our bane:
Care kills us, griefe, diseases doth outweare
This life, Death dragges us to the dolefull bierre.
Fortune takes what she in the morning gave,
Or enemies robbe and spoile what e're we have;
Strength, beauty perish, honours flye away,
False friends, when meanes are gone, they will not stay;
Hope's onely constant in adversity,
Before she's kil'd by death, she will not fly.

Lychnocausia...Lights, Morall Emblems, etc. 1638

FELLTHAM

OWEN FELLTHAM (1602?–1668). Chaplain, or perhaps
secretary and tutor, in Northamptonshire. His first work
appeared in 1620, *Resolves: Divine, Morall, Politicall*. These
are a hundred short essays on various subjects. They
were very popular and the eighth edition in 1661 contained
also thirty-nine poems called *Lusoria, or Occasional Pieces*.

CONTENTMENT

TRANSLATION FROM MARTIAL

THINGS that can bless a life, and please,
 Sweetest Martial, they are these:
 A store well left, not gain'd with toil,
A house thine own, and pleasant soyl;
No strife, small state, a mind at peace,
Free strength, and limbs free from disease;
Wise Innocence, friends like and good,
Unarted-meat, kind neighbourhood;
No drunken rest, from cares yet free,
No sadning spouse, yet chaste to thee;
Sleeps, that long nights abbreviate;
Because 'tis liking, thy wish't state;
Nor fear'd, nor joy'd, at death or fate.

Resolves: Divine, Morall, Politicall
(Eighth impression), 1661

THE SUN AND WIND

WHY think'st thou, fool, thy Beautie's rayes
    Should flame my colder heart,
When thy disdain shall several wayes
    Such piercing blasts impart?

Seest not those beams that guild the day,
    (Though they be hot and fierce),
Yet have not heat nor power to stay,
    When winds their strength disperse.

So, though thy Sun heats my desire,
    Yet know thy coy disdain
Falls like a storm on that young fire,
    So blowes me cool again.

Ibid.

THE SYMPATHY

SOUL of my soul! it cannot be
    That you should weep, and I from tears be free.
    All the vast room between both Poles
      Can never dull the sense of souls
        Knit in so fast a knot.
    Oh! can you grieve, and think that I
    Can feel no smart because not nigh
        Or that I know it not?

    Th'are heretick thoughts. Two Lutes are strung
And on a Table tun'd alike for song;
    Strike one, and that which none did touch
    Shall, sympathizing, sound as much

As that which toucht you see.   *Felltham*
Think then this world, which Heaven inroules,
Is but a Table round, and souls
    More apprehensive be.

Know they, that in their grossest parts
Mix, by their hallowed loves, intwined hearts,
    This privilege boast, that no remove
    Can e're infringe their sense of love.
        Judge hence then our estate,
Since when we lov'd there was not put
Two earthen hearts in one brest, but
        Two souls Co-animate.

                                    Ibid.

A FAREWELL

WHEN by sad fate from hence I summon'd am,
    |Call it not Absence, that's too mild a name.
    Believe it, dearest Soul, I cannot part,
For who can live two Regions from his heart
Unlesse, as stars direct our humane sense,
I live by your more powerful influence?
No: say I am dissolv'd: for, as a Cloud
By the Sun's vigour melted is, and strow'd
On the Earth's face, to be exhal'd again
To the same beams that turn'd it into rain,
So absent think me but as scatter'd dew,
Till re-exhal'd again to Vertue—You.

                                    Ibid.

Felltham

AN EPITAPH
ON THE LADY MARY FARMOR

CHASTELY to live, one husband wed, he gone,
   Gravely to spend a Widowhood alone;
   Full seventeen tedious years in memory
Of that dear worth which dy'd when he did dye;
To make life one long act of goodnesse; gain
More love than the world's malice e're could stain;
Then calmly passe with sighs of every friend,
Were those brave wayes which her so much commend
That 'tis no strong Line but a Truth, to fix,
"Here lies the best Example of her Sex".

Ibid.

ON A HOPEFUL YOUTH

STAY, Passenger, and lend a tear,
   Youth and Vertue both lye here.
   Reading this, know thou hast seen
Virtue tomb'd at but Fifteen.
And if after thou shalt see
Any young and good as he,
Think his vertues are reviving
For Examples of thy living.
Practise those and then thou maist
Fearlesse dye where now thou stay'st.

Ibid.

TO PHRYNE

Felltham

WHEN thou thy youth shalt view
    Fam'd out, and hate thy glass for telling true;
    When thy face shall be seen
        Like to an Easter Apple gathered green;
When thy whole body shall
    Be one foul wrinkle, lame and shrivell'd all
So deep, that men therein
    May find a grave to bury shame and sin;
When no claspt youth shall be
    Pouring his bones into his lap and thee;
When thy own wanton fires
    Shall leave to bubble up thy loose desires;
Then wilt thou sighing lye,
    Repent and smart, and so by two deaths dye.

Ibid.

UPON A RARE VOICE

WHEN I but hear her sing, I fare
    Like one that, raised, holds his ear
    To some bright star, in the supremest Round;
    Through which, besides the light that's seen,
    There may be heard from Heaven within,
The Rests of Anthems that the Angels sound.

Ibid.

FETTIPLACE

THOMAS FETTIPLACE (1600?–1670). A student of medicine. His only book was *The Sinner's Tears, in Meditations and Prayers*, 1653. It is almost entirely in prose.

THE SINNER'S COMPLAINT

AH, Lord, so long! What sudden fears,
What cares and doubts, what sighs and teares,
Since last thou did'st afford thy loving look
  Have me oprest
  And rob'd of rest,
Because thou, Lord, thy servant hast forsook?

If not a look, yet hear me speak
And pittie me. O do not break
Thy bruised reed: why should'st thou strive with man,
  Whose dayes are done
  When but begun,
Sith thou, great God, hast measur'd out his span?

Amaze me not with fearfull things;
Give me thy grace, O give me wings
Of swift desire and holy zeal, to raise
  My soul to skies
  With powerfull cryes,
That I may sweetly warble forth thy praise.

Thou art my Centre; fix me there,
Or move me in thy blessed Sphere;
Suffer me not, dear Lord, to moove from thee;
  There is no nest
  But in thy Brest,
And in thine absence present misery.

O that I were at rest with thee,   *Fettiplace*
Or else that thou wert come to mee,
Since in thine absence I am so distrest!
        Thy wrathfull frown
        Hath thrown me down,
And rais'd a storm in my unquiet brest.

Come, Lord, and close these wretched eyes,
So blear'd with sins and miseries;
Resolve this erring heart to tamer dust,
        Which every day
        Thus steals away,
That it may rise more joyfull and more just.

The Sinner's Tears, in Meditations and Prayers, 1653

THE SINNER'S JOY

Ah, my Soul! Why so dismai'd?
    Why so sad, so sore afraid?
    Canst thou think those gratious eyes,
      Drench'd in tears for thee,
Can disdain such powerfull cryes,
      Such humility?
Sinners' soules must sorrow keep,
Man may mourn when God can weep.

Soul, though thou hast done amiss,
Yet rejoyce, for thou art his.
See, his soul was sad to death
      In his agony,
Sad to ease thy wofull breath
      In thy misery.
Be not faithless, but beleeve
Man can sigh when God can grieve.

〈 89 〉

Fettiplace

Do not grudge to lend a tear;
Can'st thou doubt, or can'st thou fear?
Can'st thou see his bleeding heart
    And not beleeve him?
Wounded soul that bears a part
    Can never grieve him?
Timely tears are precious seed;
Men may weep when God can bleed.

Be not so cast down; alas!
See his soul forsaken was;
Frighted with his Father's frown,
    Left in paines of hell.
Ah! why art thou so cast down?
    'Twas to make thee well.
Doubt not, but admire his cost;
Man may stray when God was lost.

Soul, when thou art left alone,
Do not deem thy Saviour gone
When thou can'st not see his face;
    'Tis to let thee know
That those sinnes withdraw his grace
    Which brought him so low.
See where he in grave doth lie;
Man may faint when God can die.

Weep no more, but wipe thine eyes;
See, O see, thy Saviour rise!
Happie Soul, thy debts are paid,
    He is ascended.
Death is not; be not afraid,
    All woes are ended.
Grieve no more, believe and live;
Man may take when God can give.

Ibid.

DEO SALVATORI *Fettiplace*

WITH sighing Soul and bended knee,
Thy Servant vows himself to Thee:
My God, accept a broken heart
Bleeding for Sin; O thou which art
The Soveraign balm, vouchsafe to bee
(My dearest Lord), that Balm to mee.
Inlighten, with thy saving grace,
Those eyes thou guidest to this place,
And grant (dear God) those sins of mine
May not obscure that Grace of thine.

Ibid.

FLETCHER

THOMAS FLETCHER (1667–1713). Fellow of New College, Oxford, and master at Winchester. His only volume of verses was published in 1692, *Poems on several Occasions, and translations: Wherein the First and Second Books of Virgil's Aeneis are attempted, in English*. He had interesting views on translation and on prosody.

CONTENT

A PASTORAL DIALOGUE

Thyrsis. By your Pipe's leave, good Damon, say,
(If thou canst ought but sing and play),
Why, when all the Swains complain,
These of Drought, and those of Rain,
Some that Ewes unnat'ral prove,
Some pine for Envy, some for Love,
Only thou, of all the Swains,
With Songs and Smiles divert'st the Plains?
Say, my gentle Shepherd, say,
Why art thou so blith and gay?
Damon. Rather, Shepherd, tell me, why,
If Swains will be fools, must I
Play the fool for Company?
Swains unwisely do complain,
Some of Drought, and some of Rain;
They may thank themselves for what's amiss:
They make their own Unhapiness.
Some wish and see their Flocks increase;
They gain Wealth, but lose their Peace:
Folds enlarg'd enlarge their care;

Who have much, for much must fear;   *Fletcher*
Others see their flocks decay;
With their flocks they pine away.
The Shepherd who would happy be,
Must not seek Causes for his Joy;
Must not for Pretences tarry;
But be unreasonably merry.
    Thyrsis. But, Damon, if thy Folds increase,
If Frost thy falling Lambkins seize,
Does not thy Breast with Sorrow swell?
    Damon. No; yet I love my Lambkins well:
Whatsoe'r by Pan is sent,
Still I think a blessing meant:
If he will retrench my store,
He takes but what he gave before.
Life's an art, and Happiness
A Knack, which Swains may learn with ease.
    Thyrsis. Ah! gentle Shepherd! only show
How I may blest and happy grow.
This Sheep-Crook, which I long have kept,
See! 'tis rich wood, and finely shap'd!
'Twas good Menalcas' Legacy,
When he left the World and me;
(Damon that falling tear forgive,
Menalcas did deserve my Grief);
He the pretty Sheep-Crook gave,
Which oft did my Lycoris crave;
Oft she crav'd, but ne'er could gain:
Yet show me this and it is thine.
    Damon. I too can boast t'have shar'd a part,
When time was, in Menalcas' Heart.
And, Thyrsis, for his sake I'll show,
How thou may'st blest and happy grow;

⟨ 93 ⟩

Fletcher Yet thou shalt keep thy Sheep-Crook too.
Not that I pretend to be
From Troubles or from Passions free;
But still my thoughts I fasten there,
Where I find least ground for Care.
Heav'n wisely tempers Humane Life,
Wisely mingles Joy and Grief.
And I still chuse to mind the best;
Let who will think upon the rest.
If frost my falling lambs destroy,
Yet my Ewes I still enjoy:
But if they should perish too,
Yet I, Methinks, were blest enow.
Still my Pipe and Verse remain;
The Poem, Alcon brag'd, was mine.
Sometimes my other Songs I've shew'd
And Shepherds seem to think they're good.
Yes! and they call me Poet too,
But I'm too wise to think it true.
Udemia, sweetest, fairest Maid!
For her these two white Kids I feed.
The Gift is hearty, tho' but small;
In Gifts the Giver's Mind is all.
For her I wish my Flock's increase;
Yet she shall never break my Peace.
I'm blest enough, if kind she prove;
If not, she do'nt deserve my Love.
  Thyrsis. Hold a while, good Damon, hold!
Yonder Ram has broke the Fold.
'Tis a cross unlucky thing;
Go there, Lightfoot, fetch him in!
Shepherd, now resume thy Lays,
And I'll crown thy head with Bays.

Damon. If tuneful Birds salute the Spring,   *Fletcher*
From the Birds I learn to sing;
If the Heavens laugh awhile,
From the Heav'ns I learn to smile:
But if Mists obscure the Day,
And black Clouds fright the Sun away;
I never dread the angry Sky;
Why should I think it frowns on me?
I to my peaceful Cell retreat;
Yonder see the homely Seat!
'Tis what Nature did provide;
(Nature I ever make my Guide).
There I sit and there I play,
Cheat my Cares and Hours away:
Reflect on honest Pleasures past,
Or which I shall hereafter tast:
Think on the Time when I shall be
From Clouds and Storms for ever free,
Plac'd in Elysium; where, they say,
Blest Ghosts enjoy Eternal Day,
Eternal Spring; where all the year,
The Fields their freshest Honours wear.
So I heard old Sophron say;
I heard, and almost wished to die.
In vain the sullen Heavens scowl,
Storms and Tempests round me howl;
I make fair weather in my Soul:
All Occasions I embrace,
Which may give me Joy and Peace;
And drive bad Objects from my Thought;
What can't be cured, is best forgot.
Now say, my honest Thyrsis, say,
Why should I not be blith and gay?

⟨ 95 ⟩

                    Thyrsis. Be ever blith, be ever gay;
                 Pan reward thy Courtesie;
                 Blessings on thy Pipe, and thee!
                 Health to thy Flock, Peace to thy Mind;
                 And be thy lov'd Eudemia kind.

*Poems on several Occasions.
and translations,* 1692

SONG

OH, Ecstasie Divine! I cannot hold!
     Farewel, dull Earth! See where my ravish'd Soul
     Stands shiv'ring on the edge of its slow Clay!
With the next rising Note 'twill fly away.
I faint; I faint. The pow'rful Charm forbear!
Nay, but sing on: sure that will keep it here.
Whither, fond Soul, ah, whither would'st thou fly?
To Heav'n? Can there be sweeter Harmony?
'Tis strange the Charms of Harmony which give
To all things Life, should make me cease to live.
Yet is this Death? If it be thus to die,
Death cannot be a Curse; or, if it be,
Ye angry Pow'rs, may't ever light on me.

Ibid.

ON A LADY'S PICTURE

BELIEVE, Posterity, believe it true
     This from no fancied Form the Pencil drew;
     No Angel sat with lucid Visions sent
To bless the Eyes of some departing Saint.
No, all the Charms which on this Picture dwell,
(And ah! what pity 'tis), were mortal all.

⟨ 96 ⟩

Thus much 'tis fit to let the Picture speak   *Fletcher*
Lest this for some bright Being they mistake
Of Heav'nly Race; and to Mankind be lost
The greatest Honour it could ever boast.

                                                                        Ibid.

THE IMPATIENT

ENOUGH, enough of this world's fruitless Care
    And even its Pleasures I have suffer'd here;
    I'm weary of Life's gross Hypocrisie,
With Plenty starv'd, cloy'd with Variety.
Oh happy, happy State, when shall I be
From fancy'd Good and real Evil free?
When one short, well-spent Sigh shall me remove
From all the Cheats mistaken Mortals love:
When undeceiv'd by fancied shadows, I
Shall very Beauty in its Fountain see!
Oh, happy, happy State! Why do I stay?
Move faster, Time, how slowly dost thou fly,
As if the weight of Years had crippled thee!
Thou, Death's Procurer, quickly bring me safe
Into the cold Embraces of the Grave;
There shall I blest, at least shall quiet lie
Till the Angelick Summons from on High
Call me to Bliss and real Life away:
Then shall devouring Flame with fury hurled
Revenge my quarrel on the injurious World;
Then thou shalt cease and Death himself shall die;
And both together lost and bury'd lie,
He in eternal Life and thou in vast Eternity.

                                                                        Ibid.

GOULD

ROBERT GOULD (1660?–1709?). Dramatist and poet. His most popular poem, which evoked many replies, was *Love given o're*, 1683, a satire against women. He also attacked Presbyterianism, love of wealth and love-making. His verse tragedies are worthless. His *Poems, chiefly consisting of Satyrs and Satyrical Epistles*, 1689, shows that he could write a capable late-Restoration love-song.

SONG

THE CAUTION

AH Silvia! have a Care—that Glance
    Alas! belong'd to me;
    Ev'n tho' thy Eyes but rov'd by Chance
    'Twould yet Injustice be.
I should not care indeed if thine
    Did but like common Beauties move;
But ah! those lights can never shine
    Without inspiring Love.

What conquer'd me, alas! my Dear,
    Will others conquer too:
In vain you cry, I need not fear,
    And promise to be true.
If you are pleas'd when e'er you make
    Some other youthful Heart your Prize,
Your Love its flight will quickly Take,
    And wait upon your Eyes.

*Poems, chiefly consisting of Satyrs
and Satyrical Epistles*, 1689

WIT AND BEAUTY

WHEN from her Beauty long I've strove
      To free my doating Heart,
   Her wit brings back my fliting Love,
      And chains it down by Art.

Then, when her wit I've often foil'd,
      With one commanding view,
I'm by her Eyes again beguil'd,
      And Captive took anew.

Her Wit alone were vain, alone
      Her Beauty would not do;
But what the Devil can be done
      With Wit and Beauty too?

Ibid.

HAGTHORPE

JOHN HAGTHORPE (*fl.* 1622, alive in 1630?). A lesser poet of some ability who published some verses in 1622 and four other poems in 1623. He may have been the Captain John Hagthorpe, whose name frequently occurs in the State Papers of the reign of Charles I. The first book was *Divine Meditations and Elegies* and the second *Visiones Rerum, The vision of things, or foure poems.* Hagthorpe has a pleasing fancy and some of the Elizabethan capacity for using proper names.

AN ELEGIE UPON THE DEATH OF THE MOST
ILLUSTRIOUS PRINCE HENRIE

I DOE not grieve when some unwholesome aire
   Mildewes rich fields; nor when the clusters faire
   Of Claret rot through too abundant showers:
I grieve not when some gay unsavoury flowers
Are nipt and wither'd by th'untimely frost.
   Onely herin my patience suffers most,
When the sweet Harvest and expected gaine
   Of Vertue's Vintage, ere full ripe is slaine:
When Time the Wheat with cruell scythe cuts downe,
   But leaves such vulgar weeds as are unmowne,
Darnell and Vetches: when these mortall lights
   Extinguisht be, should guide our dimmer sights,
Then, then I weepe, and wish the watry clouds
   Would furnish me with teares to weepe whole flouds.
Then wish I Boreas, (whose killing breath
   Is ne'er perfum'd with sweets of Indian Earth),
To lend me sighs. I wish the Culver's groanes,
   The Pellican's shrill shrikes to expresse my moanes.
I wish my selfe those Dedalean wings,
   To search the glorious Courts of th'Easterne Kings:

And a strong Pattent seal'd from powerfull Love,   *Hagthorpe*
   Freely to take all that my thoughts approve.
First would I then in Indian forests slit
   The weeping Plant, (with Ivorie Knife), to get
Such pretious liquor uncorrupted cleare,
   As might embalme heroyck Henrie here.
Then would I next to Tauris' gardens pierce
   For rarest flowers to strew upon his Hearse:
Th'Indies should yeeld us Diamonds, China, Gold;
   Perue that silver that her lap doth hold;
Sylon and Ormus, all their Pearle should send,
   The Congian Slaves from secret caves should rend
The Chyan Marble, white Cassidonie,
   Greene Lacedemon, and red Porpherie.
The pure white Marble got in Palestine,
   And rare Numidian, spotted Serpentine.
Tuskane should yeeld me then some Architect,
   Whose artfull wit should first these Stones dissect
With Sand and toothlesse Saw; and then engrave
   What stories there you memoriz'd would have.
Which worke let mine imagination frame
   So large, that the whole Earth might seeme to
      th'same
A fitting Basis, whence a loftie Spire,
   Through the triple airie Regions, and much higher,
Should penetrate: so should the whole Earth be
   His tombe, and the fair Heavens his Canopie.
This Piramed, a Pharos, serving right
   For to direct the storme-tost wandring Wight
To Safetie: for since Fate didst life designe,
   A patterne unto this Cimmerian time
To imitate; tho' Atropos accurst,
   His Clew, but new begun, in sunder burst,

Hagthorpe   Yet that small piece in tables Smaragdine,
          I would preserve for light therein to shine
     From there our Labyrinthian waies uneven,
          To guide us just that way he went to Heaven.

Divine Meditations and Elegies, 1622

TENTH MEDITATION

THE race of men is like the leaves of trees,
     The greatest part whereof in ditches fall,
     Or straw the dirtie earth, tost by the brize
Of wanton winds that sport themselves withall:
          Few doe they lay aloft on towres of state,
          Much fewer thence doe not precipitate.

The race of men are like the Flowers, that be
     By Nature given their mother Earth t'adorne
As well with beautie as varietie
     Of their indowments. Some have comely forme
          But little vertue: Noble some, not faire;
          Some great, but weak; some small, whose face,
               most rare,

Oft-times mis-plact. The cordiall Violet
     And fragrant Rose in ditch or high-way side:
And Henbane, and Cicuta ranke, unset,
     In fairest gardens, are not seldome spied.
          But most in this do we resemble Flowers;
          We spring, we flourish, wither in few houres.

The race of men are like the scalie traine,
     Of nimble Fish, in silver Iourdan's streame,
That while they follow prey or sportfull game,
     (Ignorant of the danger nearest them),
          Fall with the sliding waves, that swiftly flie
          Into the Mare Mortuum, and die.

The world's a streame, most pleasing to our eres,   *Hagthorpe*
    But from our sights much faster, swifter gliding,
Then Iourdain to the Mare Mortuum flies;
    The Fish are men, that in the same are biding,
        Who while in Pleasure's streames they bathe and
            dwell,
        Are carried downe therewith, and slide to hell.

Now for the leaves and Flowers, they may accuse
    The Winds, that most their beauties doth deface.
The Fish, of apprehension most obtuse,
    May challenge Nature for their wretched case.
        But man that little lesse then Angels knowes,
        Can blame none but himselfe for all his woes.

                                                Ibid.

TO EARTH

EARTH, thou art a barren Field
        Of delight and true contenting;
    All the pleasures thou do'st yeeld,
        Give but cause of sad lamenting:
                Where desires
                Are the fires,
        Still our soules tormenting.

Riches, Honour, Dignitie,
        Are the high way to misfortune:
Greatnesse is a lethargie,
        That to death can soone transport one.
                To be faire,
                Causeth care,
        Gifts chaste thoughts importune.

⟨ 103 ⟩

Hagthorpe

To be wittie, quick of tongue,
    Sorrow to themselves returneth.
To be Healthfull, Young and Strong,
    Feeds the flames where passion burneth:
        Yet doe Men
        Covet them,
    More than what adorneth.

To have Friends, and Lovers kind,
    That us round environ:
Wife and Children, tho we find
    These be robes that best attire one,
        Yet their losse,
        Is a crosse,
    Melting hearts of Iron.

To be perfect here, and wise,
    Is to know our indiscretions;
And our goodnes chiefely lies,
    In observing our transgressions:
        For we dwell,
        As in Hell,
    Thrall to bad impressions.

Then, alas, why long we so,
    With lov'd Sorrow still to languish?
Is there ought on earth but woe,
    Aye renewing cares and anguish?
        Where new feares,
        Still appeares,
    Darts at us to brandish?

Ibid.

HAWKINS

HENRY HAWKINS (1571?–1646). Jesuit priest. Wrote poems, translations and lives of the saints. His *Partheneia Sacra*, published in Paris, 1633 (and perhaps earlier in Rouen in 1632), contained prose accounts of the Virgin Mary. Each is followed by short verses. Some have a quiet, simple charm.

THE VIRGIN

I. THE VIOLET

IN Heaven the humble Angels God beheld;
And on the earth, with Angels paralel'd,
The lowlie Virgin view'd. Her modest eye,
Submissive count'nance, thought that did relye
On him that would exalt an humble wight
And make his Mother Alma, ne're in sight,
With vertues, fragrant odours, round beset,
Close to the earth lay like the Violet;
Which, shrowded with its leaves, in covert lyes,
Found sooner by the sent then by the eyes.
   Such was the Virgin rays'd to be Heaven's Queene,
Who on the earth, neglected, was not seene.

*Partheneia Sacra, or the Mysterious
and Delicious Garden of the Sacred
Parthenes . . ., 1633*

THE glorious Sunne withdrew his beames of light;
My sinne was cause. So I, in dismal night,
Am sayling in a stormie dangerous Maine;
And ere the Sunne, I feare, returne againe,
Shal suffer shipwrack, where the fraite's my Soule.
My onlie Hope's a Starre, fixt neere the Pole;
But that my Needle now hath lost its force,
Once touch'd with grace, and sailes out of course.
Starre of the Sea, thy Sun hath given thee light:
Til he brings day guide me in sinne's dark night.
    I seeke what Sages heertofore have donne,
    Guided by thee, a Starre, to find the Sunne.

Ibid.

HAWKSHAW

BENJAMIN HAWKSHAW (1673–1738). Vicar in Dublin. His volume of verses was called *Poems upon Several Occasions*, 1693.

THE ADVICE

CHLOE be kind, I say;
　　Beauty has Wings as well as Time;
　　To suffer either pass away
Without Advantage, is a Crime.
See, Heav'n itself with conscious Smiles approves
The future Union of our tender Loves.

　　Then why, my Dear, should you
　　So fatal to your Beauties prove?
　　Pay unto Nature what's her due
　　And then you'l ne're refuse my Love;
Take my Advice, preserve that Vestal Fire;
When it is doubl'd it will ne're expire.

　　Sweet Chloe, hear my call,
　　And think to live no more alone;
　　Tho' Man was born as Lord of all
　　Himself but odly fills a Throne;
Eden was not compos'd of That or This,
Woman and Man made up the Paradise.

Poems upon Several Occasions, 1693

HEYRICK

THOMAS HEYRICK (1649–1694). Curate of Market Harborough in Leicestershire. Author of many, not uninteresting, sermons. His *Miscellany Poems* appeared in 1691. Most are curious but very readable. The longest is "The Submarine Voyage" which is in four short "books" of pindarics. It is fantastic but often delightful. His other poems are full of whimsical, pleasant conceits and odd fancies.

ON A SUNBEAM

I

THOU Beauteous Off-spring of a Syre as Fair,
  With thy kind Influence thou dost all things heat:
  Thou gild'st the Heaven, the Sea, the Earth and Air,
And under massy Rocks dost Gold beget.
    Th'opaque dull Earth thou dost make fine,
    Thou dost ith' Moon and Planets shine,
    And, if Astronomy say true,
Our Earth to them doth seem a Planet too.

II

How unaccountable thy Journeys prove!
Thy swift Course thro' the Universe doth fly,
From lofty heights in distant Heavens above,
To all that at the lowly Center ly.
    Thy Parent Sun once in a Day
    Thro' Heaven doth steer his well-beat way;
    Thou of a swifter, subtler breed
Dost every Moment his Day's Course exceed.

Thy Common presence makes thee little priz'd,
Which, if we once had lost, wee'd dearly Buy:
How would the Blind hugg what's by us despis'd!
How welcome wouldst thou in a Dungeon be!
  Thrice-wretched those in Mines are bred
  That from thy sight are buried,
  When all the Stores for which they try
Neither in Use, nor Beauty, equal Thee.

IV

Could there be found an Art to fix thee down,
And of condensed Rays a Gem to make,
'Twould be the brightest Lustre of a Crown,
And an esteem invaluable take.
  New Wars would the tir'd World molest,
  And new Ambition fire Men's breast,
  More Battels fought for it, than e're
Before for Love, Empire, or Treasure were.

V

Thou'rt quickly born and dost as quickly die:
Pitty so fair a Birth to fate should fall!
Now here and now in abject Dust dost lie,
One Moment 'twixt thy Birth and Funeral.
  Art thou, like Angels, only shown,
  Then, to our Grief, for ever flown?
  Tell me, Apollo, tell me where
The Sunbeams go, when they do disappear.

Miscellany Poems, 1691

Dost think He whom thy liberal Table drew,
 Can ever be to Love or Friendship true?
 He loves thy Mullets, Oysters, and not Thee:
Could I so entertain him, hee'd love Me.

Ibid.

From AN ELEGY ON THE DEATH OF LADY BUTLER

She fell an Holocaust of Chast Delight,
 Beauteous and Fair, as Rays of new-born Light.
 Charming, as Vertues i'th'Idaea be,
Or Graces, seen by th'Intellectual Eye.

Ibid.

ON AN INDIAN TOMINEIOS, THE LEAST OF BIRDS

I

I'me made in sport by Nature, when
  Shee's tir'd with the stupendious weight
 Of forming Elephants and Beasts of State;
Rhinoceros, that love the Fen;
  The Elkes, that scale the hills of Snow,
And Lions couching in their awfull Den:
  These do work Nature hard, and then
  Her wearied Hand in Me doth show
What she can for her own Diversion doe.

Man is a little World ('tis said),
    And I in Miniature am drawn,
A Perfect Creature, but in Short-hand shown.
    The Ruck, in Madagascar bred,
    (If new Discoveries Truth do speak)
Whom greatest Beasts and armed Horsemen dread,
    Both him and Me one Artist made:
    Nature in this Delight doth take,
That can so Great and Little Monsters make.

III

The Indians me a Sunbeam name,
    And I may be the Child of one:
So small I am, my Kind is hardly known.
    To some a sportive Bird I seem,
    And some believe me but a Fly;
Tho' me a Feather'd Fowl the Best esteem:
    What e're I am, I'me Nature's Gemm,
    And like a Sunbeam from the Sky,
I can't be follow'd by the quickest Eye.

IV

I'me the true Bird of Paradise,
    And heavenly Dew's my only Meat:
My Mouth so small, 'twill nothing else admit.
    No Scales know how my weight to poise,
    So Light, I seem condensed Air;
And did at th'End of the Creation rise,
    When Nature wanted more Supplies,
    When she could little Matter spare,
But in Return did make the work more Rare.   *Ibid.*

ON THE DEATH OF A MONKEY

HERE, Busy and yet Innocent, lyes Dead
  Two things that seldom meet:
 No Plots nor Stratagems disturb'd his head,
  Or's merry Soul did fret.
He shew'd, like Superannuated Peer;
Grave was his look, and Politick his Air;
And he for Nothing, too, spent all his care.

But that he died of Discontent, 'tis fear'd,
  Head of the Monkey Rout;
To see so many Brother Apes preferr'd,
  And he himself left out.
On all below he did his Anger Show'r,
Fit for a Court did all above adore,
H'had Shows of Reason, and few Men have more.

Ibid.

HOWARD

ANNE HOWARD (1557–1630). The fiercely Roman Catholic
wife of Philip Howard, first Duke of Arundel. She wrote no
verse that has survived except this elegy on the death of her
husband, which is Elizabethan in style. It is pleasant, and
interesting, if her character was as harsh and cruel as it is said
to have been, and from beneath the conventionally bucolic
strains a note of genuine feeling breaks through.

ELEGY

IN sad and ashie weeds I sigh,
    I grone, I pine, I mourne;
    My oten yellow reeds
      I all to jeat and ebon turne.
My watrie eyes, lyke winter's skyes,
    My furrowed cheeks o'reflow.
All heavens knowe why men mourne as I,
    And who can blame my woe?

In sable robes of night my dayes
    Of joye consumed be;
My sorrowe sees no light;
    My lights through sorrowe nothing see:
For now my sonne his course hath ronne,
    And from his sphere doth goe,
To endless bed of soulded lead,
    And who can blame my woe?

My flocks I nowe forsake, that soe
    My sheep my greefe may knowe;
The Lillies loth to take
    That since his death presum'd to growe.

Howard   I envie aire because it dare
                Still breath, and he not soe;
          Hate earth, that doth entombe his youth,
                And who can blame my woe?

Not I, poor I alone—(alone
          How can this sorrowe be?)
Not onely men make mone, but
          More than men make mone with me:
The gods of greenes, the mountain queenes,
          The fairy circles rowe,
The muses nine, and powers devine,
          Do all condole my woe.

From *Illustrations of British History . . . in the reigns of Henry VIII . . . James I* (Lodge), 1791

HOWARD

SIR ROBERT HOWARD (1626–1698). Cavalier, M.P., and Auditor of the Exchequer. Shadwell's "Sir Positive At-All" in *The Sullen Lovers*, 1668. Chiefly a playwright. His serious contribution to poetry was *Poems*, 1660. Best known for his collaboration with Dryden and for the part he was given in Dryden's *Essay on Dramatic Poetry*.

TO THE UNCONSTANT CYNTHIA

A SONG

TELL me once, Dear, how it does prove
    That I so much forsworn could be?
    I never swore always to love,
I onely vow'd still to love thee:
      And art thou now what thou wert then,
      Unsworn unto by other men?

In thy fair Breast, and once-fair Soul,
I thought my Vows were writ alone;
But others' Oaths so blurr'd the Scrole,
That I no more could read my own.
      And am I still oblig'd to pay
      When you had thrown the Bond away?

Nor must we onely part in Joy,
Our tears as well must be unkind:
Weep you, that could such truth destroy,
And I, that could such falseness find.
      Thus we must unconcern'd remain
      In our divided Joys and Pain.

Yet we may love, but on this diff'rent score,
You what I am, I what you were before.

Poems, 1660

⟨ 115 ⟩   8-2

TO THE SAME

Y OU are not, Cynthia, better pleased than I,
    That you first led the way
    Through this dark night of blind Inconstancy
    And first found break of Day:
To freedom now we'l sacrifice dreams past:
'Twas my good fate to cry Good-morrow last.

Perhaps so soon I could not dis-engage,
    Having a greater score.
Some Birds will longer hover round the Cage
    Though 'twas their Jayl before:
Yet sure I meant not long to sit about
The ashes, when the fire was quite burnt out.

Since now my Jaylor has my Chains unty'd,
    I'le hold my hand no more
Up at Love's Bar; he is condemn'd untride
    That has been burnt before:
Now that heart-sickness which she gave, protects:
'Tis seldom that the same plague twice infects.

Breasts that have known Love's cruell slavery
    Are better fortifi'd
By that experience, than they ere can be
    By reason or by pride.
Then blush not that you quench'd this am'rous flame
But blush with me, if we two love again.   *Ibid.*

THE RESOLUTION

N O, Cynthia, never think I can
    Love a divided heart and mind;
    Your Sunshine love to every man
Appears alike as great as kind.

None but the duller Persians kneel *Howard*
And the bright god of Beams implore,
Whilst others equall influence feel
That never did the god adore.

The riches of your Love's put forth,
And ev'ry man retains a part;
You can't Call't in to make you worth
The purchase of a faithfull heart.

Hope not to be mine, or your own;
You can't your selfe to me restore;
The nest is left, the Birds are flown,
And bankrupt-Love sets up no more.

Your kindnesse, which at randome flyes,
Makes your Love-patients all secure;
But they will find your Emp'rick eyes
Can only palliate, never cure.

Though I resolve to love no more
Since I did once, I will advise.
The love of Conquests now give o're;
Disquiets wait on Victories.

To your much-injur'd peace and name
Love's farewell as a tribute pay,
Grow now reserv'd and raise your fame
By your own choice, not your decay.

She that to Age her charms resignes
And then at last turns Votary,
Though Vertue much the change inclines,
'Tis sullied by Necessity.

Ibid.

HOWELL

JAMES HOWELL (1593–1666). He had the adventurous career of university student, "steward" in a glass factory, traveller abroad for the factory, tutor, court envoy to Spain, College Fellow, secretary to Lord Scrope, secret agent, Clerk of the Council, M.P., and Historiographer Royal. He was also imprisoned during the Commonwealth. His poems were collected and published in 1663, *Poems on Several Choice and Various Subjects, etc.* A second edition appeared, with a different title, in 1664.

A FIT OF MORTIFICATION

WEAK crazy Mortal, why dost fear
     To leave this Earthly Hemisphear,
     Where all delights away do pass
     Like thy Effigies in a Glass?
Each thing beneath the Moon is frail and fickle;
Death sweeps away what Time cuts with his sickle.

This Life at best is but an Inn,
     And we the Passengers wherein
The cloth is laid to some, before
     They peep out of Dame Nature's dore,
And warm Lodgings find. Others there are
Must trudge to find a room, and shift for fare.

This Life's at longest but one day:
     He who in Youth posts hence away
Leaves us i' th' Morn; He who hath run
     His race till Manhood, parts at Noon;
And who at seventy odd forsakes this Light
He may be said to take his leave at Night.

One paest makes up the Prince and Peasan,   *Howell*
        Though one eats roots, the other Feasan:
They nothing differ in the Stuff,
        But both extinguish like a Snuff.
Why then, fond Man, shold thy soul take dismay
To sally out of these gross walls of Clay?

> *Poems on Several Choice and Various Subjects, etc.* 1663

A RAPTURE UPON DELIA

COULD I but catch those Golden Rays
        Which Phoebus at High Noon displays,
        I'd set them on a Loom, and frame
A Scarf for Delia of the same.

Could I that wondrous black come near,
Which Cynthia, when she mourns doth wear;
Of a new fashion I wold trace
A Mask therof for Delia's face.

Could I but reach that Green and Blue,
Which Iris decks in such rare hue
From her moist Bow, I'd drag them down
To make my Celia a Summer-Gown.

Could I those Whitely Stars come nigh
Which makes the Milky-way in Sky,
I'd Poach them, and at Moon-shine dress,
To make my Delia a Hougon Mess.

Thus would I diet, thus attire
My Delia Queen of Hearts and Fire:
She shold have ev'ry thing Divine,
What might befit a Seraphine.
And 'cause ungirt unblest we often find,
One of the lesser Zones her waste shold bind.   *Ibid.*

⟨ 119 ⟩

AND is thy glasse run out? is that oil spent,
Which light to such tough sinewy labours lent?
Well, Ben, I now perceive that all the Nine,
Though they their utmost forces should combine,
Cannot prevail 'gainst Night's three daughters, but
One still spin, one wind, the other cut.
Yet in despight of spindle, clue and knife,
Thou, in thy strenuous lines, hast got a life,
Which, like thy bay, shall flourish every age,
While sock or buskin move upon the stage.

Ibid.

UPON A FIT OF DISCONSOLATION, OR DESPONDENCY OF SPIRIT

EARLY and late, both night and day,
By Moon-shine and the Sun's bright Ray,
When spangling Stars emboss'd the Sky
And deck'd the World's vast Canopy,
    I sought the Lord of Life and Light,
    But, oh, my Lord kept out of sight.

As at all times, so ev'ry Place
I made my Church to seek his Face,
In Forests, Chases, Parks and Woods,
On Mountains, Meadows, Fields and Floods,
    I sought the Lord of Life and Light,
    But still my Lord kept out of sight.

On Neptune's back, when I could see   *Howell*
But few pitch'd planks 'twixt Death and me,
In Freedom and in Bondage long,
With Groans and Cries, with Pray'r and Song,
    I sought the Lord of Life and Light,
    But still my Lord kept out of sight.

In Chamber, Closet, (swoln with Tears),
I sent up Vows for my Arrears;
In Chappel, Church and Sacrament,
(The Soul's Ambrosian Nourishment),
    I sought the Lord of Life and Light,
    But still my Lord kept out of sight.

What? is mild Heaven turn'd to Brass,
That neither sigh nor sob can pass?
Is all Commerce 'twixt Earth and Sky
Cut off from Adam's Progeny?
    That thus the Lord of Life and Light
    Should so, so long, keep out of sight?

Such Passions did my mind assail,
Such terrours did my spirits quail,
When lo, a beam of Grace shot out
Through the dark clouds of sin and doubt,
    Which did such quickning sparkles dart,
    That pierc'd the centre of my heart.

O, how my spirits came again,
How evry cranny of my brain
Was fill'd with heat and wonderment,
With joy and ravishing content,
    When thus the Lord of Life and Light
    Did re-appear unto my sight!

Learn, Sinners, hence, 'tis nere too late
To knock and cry at Heaven's gate;
That Begger's bless'd who doth not faint,
But re-inforceth still his plaint.
> The longer that the Lord doth hide his Face,
> More bright will be his after-beams of Grace.

Ibid.

TO MRS E. B.

UPON A SUDDEN SURPRISAL

APELLES, Prince of Painters, did
All others in that Art exceed,
But you surpass him, for He took
Some pains and Time to draw a Look.
> You in a trice and moment's space
> Have Pourtray'd in my Heart your Face.

Ibid.

JENKYN

PATHERICKE JENKYN (1639, *fl.* 1661). His only volume of verse was *Amorea, the Lost Lover...Being Poems, Songs, Odes, Pastorals, Elegies, Lyrick Poems and Epigrams,* 1661

TO AMOREA, THE DEDICATION

To the fairest and divine,
 Next unto the Sacred Nine,
 To the Queen of love and beauty,
I do offer up my duty;
To the sweetest disposition,
That e're Lover did petition,
To the best and happiest fortune,
Ever man did yet importune,
To the Lady of all hearts,
That pretend to noble parts;
To the altar of her eyes
I my self doe sacrifice;
To her ever winning glances,
Here I doe present my fancies;
  And to her all-commanding look
  I doe dedicate my book.

Amorea, the Lost Lover, 1661

LOVE AND RESPECT

It is not that I love thee, fairest,
 Less than when my love I tender'd,
But 'twas hopeless love, my dearest,
 That my deep affection hinder'd.

Jenkyn

Yet 'tis not hopeless love shall fear me,
　　Or command my love to end,
'Tis the high respect I bear thee,
　　Will not leave me to offend.

Were I confident to carry
　　Thy affection, it would be
No content at all to marry,
　　If the conquest were not free.

But if you vouchsafe to pardon
　　My presumption, do but prove,
I will render thee the guerdon
　　Of a never-dying love.

Ibid.

ON THE DEATH OF HIS MISTRESS

Aske me not why the Rose doth fade,
　　Lillies look pale, and Flowers die,
　　Question not why the Mirtle shade,
Her wonted shadows doth denie.

Seek not to know from whence begun
　　The sadness of the Nightingale,
Nor why the Helletrope and Sun,
　　Their constant Amitie do fail.

The Turtle's grief look not upon,
　　Nor why the Palm-tree doth mourn,
When widow-like they're left alone,
　　Nor Phoenix, why her self doth burn.

For she is dead which life did give
　　Unto those things that here I name,
They fade, change, wither, cease to live,
　　Pine, and consume into a flame.

Ibid.

⟨ 124 ⟩

TO THE SUN

Jenkyn

GOE, Glorious Sun,
>> Set in perpetual night;
>> I shun thy light;
Now she is gone
>> In whom all joyes did shine,
>>> My darkened sight
>> Can see no thing that is divine.

Goe, Glorious Sun,
>> And tell her brighter Ray
>> I come away;
Tell her I run,
>> My coming is not far:
>>> The message can be done
>> By none but thee unto a Starr.

Ibid.

KNEVET

RALPH KNEVET (1600–1671). Tutor or chaplain to the famous Norfolkshire Pastons. Became rector of Lyng. All his writings that are known are in verse: *Stratisticon, or a Discourse of Militarie Discipline, etc.* 1628; a pastoral for the Florists' Feast of Norfolk, 1631 (a long speech therein by Clematis, servant to the "new-fangl'd Lady Eglantine", is of great interest to the student of seventeenth-century dress and cosmetics); three undistinguished funeral elegies, 1637. Far better than all these are his MS. poems: *To the Honorable Sir Robert Paston's Lady; A Gallery to the Temple*; etc. Most of these are modelled on the poems of George Herbert, but they are sincere and, often, surprisingly modern in thought.

SCIENCES

MANY their language labour to correct,
And for to speake in the best dialect;
    But few, or none, contend,
    Their lives t'amend.

Logicke, the art of reason, others love,
But by their lives their studies they disprove,
    Guided by appetite,
    Not Reason's light.

Some divide numbers by Arithmeticke
To smallest fractions; yet they want a tricke
    One penny to divide
    To those that need.

Another by Geometry, (at pleasure),
Both Cittye's feilds and provinces can measure,
    Yet in his life, (God knowes),
    No measure showes.

One studyes the accord of pleasant sounds,
While in his heart with discord Hee abounds;
    Hee's out of tune within,
    Through his vaine sinne.

Th'Astrologer doth gaze upon the Starres,
Till, like a falling starre, he unawares
    In a pitt plunged is
    That's bottomless.

Another boasts diseases all to cure,
Yet findes not his owne pulse or temp'rature;
    His Heart a Spittle is
    Of maladyes.

Of Troy and Thebes th' Historian can discourse,
Of Alexander Great, and of his horse,
    Yet doth a babe become
    In things at home.

Another doth professe law to dispense,
But gives no law to his owne conscience;
    He cares more for a fee
    Then equitye.

The Theologians rather strive to know
God's will, then doe the same. Their actions grow
    Contrary to their speech
    And what they preach.

Most studye sciences, not charity,
Which is 'twixt God and Man the perfect tye.
    Oh Lord, instruct mee how
    To love, and know.

                Addit. MS. Brit. Mus. 27447

SECURITYE

TH'UNACTIVE Element
    In Man is most predominant;
    Earth is his belov'd home and his content;
        Hee well could heavenly gloryes want
If Hell or Death did not him sometimes fright.
He feares the grave, though Earth bee his delight.

    Yet Hee lives as if Hell
    Were but a fable or a storye,
A place of fancye that might parallel
    The old St Patricke's Purgatory.
Hee mirth recrutes with cups, and seldome thinkes
Of Death, untill into the grave Hee sinkes.

    But if vaine Man knew well
    To fixe and manage his designe,
Hee should not stand in feare of Death or Hell;
    For Hee's immortall and divine.
Flesh is his clogge, which while Hee strives to lighten,
More heavy growes: thus Hee his woes doth heighten.

Ibid.

THE BANKRUPTE

GOD, with the breath of life did mee inspire
    And in the world mee landed, where
    I, like a stranger, could but things admire,
    Being unfitt for pratticke there.
For I of language had not the least tittle,
    Could neither call for drinke or bread;
But when I grew acquainted but a little
    And could without a Truckman trade,

Then I forgott my home, and did neglect   *Knevet*
  Th'Imployment I was sent about;
I forraine pleasures then 'gan to affect,
  And like unthrifty Factours sought;
Not my Lord's profite, but mine owne delight.
  Both wine and women did mee please;
The women of the land were faire to sight,
  And made mee leave my busynes.
My Lord did then of my Debauchments heare,
  And to a strict account mee brought,
But I could not responsible appeare,
  I so extremely had runne out.
Then I imprisonment and bonds did feare,
  And like a perplex'd Caitife stood,
Untill a friend did whisper in mine eare
  And told mee that my Lord was good.
Hee mee advis'd to sue for mercy. Then
  I fell downe prostrate at his feet,
Which, with my teares, to bathe I did beginne,
  Th'unfained signes of my regreet.
My gracious Lord did then my debt remitt,
  Nor did his goodnes end in this,
For Hee to mee more treasures did committ,
  And more esteem'd commodityes
Then Hee with mee before intrusted had.
  Thus I who was his wretched Debtour,
His Beneficiarye blest was made,
  And then resolv'd to serve him better.

                                                    Ibid.

THE VOTE

THE Helmett now an hive for Bees becomes,
And hilts of swords may serve for Spiders' loomes;
Sharp pikes may make
Teeth for a rake;
And the keene blade, th'arch enemy of life,
Shall bee digraded to a pruneing knife.
The rusticke spade
Which first was made
For honest agriculture, shall retake
Its primitive imployment, and forsake
The rampire's steep
And trenches deep.
Tame conyes in our brazen gunnes shall breed,
Or gentle Doves their young ones there shall feede.
In musket barrells
Mice shall raise quarrells
For their quarters. The ventriloquious drumme
Like Lawyers in vacations shall be dumme.
Now all recrutes,
(But those of fruites),
Shall bee forgott; and th'unarm'd Soldier
Shall onely boast of what Hee did whilere,
In chimneys' ends
Among his freinds.

If good effects shall happy signes ensue,
I shall rejoyce, and my prediction's true.

Ibid.

TRUTH

Faire, naked Amazon,
    Invincible in force,
    Earth's Martyr, but Heaven's Minion,
Religion's Source,
The Mistris of the intellect,
A Mistris without blemish or defect.

    Great Monosyllable,
    The large Epitome
Of bookes innumerable
    That honest be,
Elder then Time thou art, yet Youth
Doth flourish in thy lookes: Thy name is Truth.

    Thy Habitation is
    In some abstruse recesse,
Not obvious to the facultyes
    Of infirme crests,
Nor yet to sense, although she trye
To reach thee by the pole of phantasye.

    Sciences, without thee,
    Are tales of Robin Hood,
No more then dreames of Fairyes bee;
    Nothing is good
Where Thou art absent, but thy presence
Gives worth, and reputation to each essence.

    Commerce is, without Thee,
    Mere Cousenage and warre,
Nothing but a grand larcenye;
    Thy vertues are
Incomputable, and thy beauty
From Men and Angels chalengeth love's duety.

Knevet

Democritus Thee hidde
In a darke, gloomy roome;
But once, I know, Thou didst proceede
From the pure wombe
Of an unviolated Mayde,
When that a Starre thy birth to Kings bewray'd.

In little Bethleem
Thou then didst shew thy face,
And after, like the Spanish streame,
Thou for a space
Layst hid in Nazareth, untill
The Lord made thee appear on Sion Hill.

To sweet Mount Olivet
The King of Truth and Peace
Did oftentimes, with his, retreate;
A fitt recesse
For Him and for his contemplations,
Who th' Herald was of peace unto all Nations.

Hee was the Word of Truth,
The light of Veritye,
Which it self disperst from his mouth
Both farre and nigh;
And though Hee our Horizon left,
Yet of his rayes wee were not quite bereft.

For though from us Hee went,
Hee left us not alone,
But downe His Holy Spirit sent
From his high Throne.
This is that Truth of truths and peace
Wherein consists our hopes and happynes.

Ibid.

THE APPARITION

Knevet

(A TRUE FRENCH STORYE)

THREE joccund Gallants in their golden age,
Count Cock'rells, in their pucillage of witt,
(For yet Discretion had not bedded it,)
Rode to the forrest in faire equipage,
Where, haveing pleas'd their phantasyes, at least,
With chase and quarry, they their sport surceast,
And curious were to find out new delights,
To cocker their fastidious appetites.
But while they view'd th'unartificiall bowres,
Which old Sylvanus for his Faunes and Satyres
Had there erected, over cristall waters,
Whose banks were diaper'd with fragrant flowres,
Their owne felicityes they call'd to mind,
Which in this sonnett sweet they thus combin'd.

"Behold our youthfull yeares,
With strength and beauty crown'd,
While Fortune faire appeares,
And richesse doe abound.
Now while the Fates permitt,
Wee our delights pursue,
And for all pleasures fitt,
Our joyes we still renue;
Which on our bosomes flow
As thicke as flights of snow."

But when these Yonkers finish'd had their song,
The scene was chang'd, for they did there descry
Three naked fabrickes of mortality,
Three horrid Sceletons, arm'd with sithes long,
Who with sad, hollow accents did repeate
This answere to those Monsieurs' canzonett.

"We liv'd in time of yore,
  And were as brave as you,
  Enrich'd with fortune's store,
  But see what wee are now!
  In us see and perpend
  Your fraile and wretched state,
  And how you must descend
  To the darke House of Fate,
  Where yee must become foode,
  Unto Earth's footles broode."

The Gallants, frighted with this apparition,
To holy vowes their gamesome humours chang'd.
This dreadfull spectacle their minds estrang'd
From secular delights and that condition
Wherein they whilome liv'd; for Eache forsooke
The World, and to a cell himself betooke.

Ibid.

INFIRMITYE

I WANT a volubility of tongue
  To trafficke for applause,
  Although I know the lawes
And rights of rhetoricke. I am not strung
  For sound and music shrill.
  My tongue's a silent quill
My witt is dumbe and doth rehearse
Things by mere signes and characters.

But my defect in this mercuriall part
  Doth chiefly mee afflict
  When I my self addict
To praise my Godd with a devoted heart.

I covet not a tongue
    To tune a wanton song,
A tongue tipp'd with deceite or guile,
A tongue to rayle or to revile.

But such a tongue I would desire to have
    As might impresse remorse
    In holy Auditoures,
And rather cause them to lamente, then laugh.
    Yet alwayes would I not
    Unto a tragicke note
My organe sett, but would make gladd
(As time should serve) a spirit sad.

Then since my tongue is so infirme, Oh Lord,
    That I cannot aspire
    To be one of thy quire,
Vouchsafe those gifts unto my heart t'afford,
    Which may make recompense
    For my tongue's impotence.
Then I shall praise Thee while my will
My tongue's defects shall cover still.

Ibid.

THE DELIVERANCE

ONE blindfold went, upon the narrow ridge
        Of a steepe bridge,
        Which with an arched bitte did curle and chappe
            A fomeing flood.
Hee, haveing pass'd along, free from mishap,
        Threw off his hood,
And looking on the danger Hee had scap't,
With infinite amazement Hee was rap't.

〈 135 〉

Knevet   Then conscious of that Providence sublime,
                      Which at that time
      Had him preserved from the jawes of Hell,
                      Immediately
      In humble sort, upon his knees Hee fell,
                      And zealously
      No dry devotions did to him forth powre
      Who from those waters deepe did him secure.

Ibid.

DEVOTION

WHILE that my knees do bowe unto my
           God
        And my officious tongue doth pray,
My heart seduced by some fancies odde,
        Doth wander quite another way.
Lord, chaine my heart, with fear and love,
That it may not at random rove.

Ibid.

THE MISTAKE

WEE blame the times,
        But doe not on our selves reflect
          To view our crimes;
And Sinne, the chiefest architect
        Of our disasters,
Our optickes tend to distance,
        And wee are Masters
Which things at Home do not redresse;

But all our losses   *Knevet*
Unto our neighbours wee impute,
    Although our crosses
Wee daily by our sinnes recrute.

If Each would seeke himself t'amend,
How soone our miseryes should end.

Ibid.

THE HABITATION

MAN is no Microcosme, and they detract
        From his dimensions, who apply
        This narrow terme to his immensitye.
            Heaven, Earth and Hell in him are pack't.
Hee's a miscellanye of goods and evills,
A Temper mixt with Angells, Beasts and Devills.

Yea! the immortall Deitye doth daigne
        T'inhabite in a carnall cell.
So pretious gemmes in the darke center dwell,
        So gloomy mines fine gold retaine.
But by vicissitudes these Essences
The various heart of Man wont to possesse.

For God no Innemate will with Satan bee:
        Angells will not consort with Beasts.
If Man would pursue his best interests,
        What blessed seasons might Hee see!
But Hee invites the Devill and the Beast,
Nor God nor Angells will Hee lodge or feast.

Ibid.

M AN in the wombe is but a Zoophyte,
    There nourish'd like a plant;
    But when Hee is produc'd to the daylight,
      Disclos'd from that warme haunte,
  Hee at the honour doth arrive
  To bee a creature sensitive.

And Memorye with Fancye in him raigne,
    Till Time makes him mature;
Then Reason settes her throne up in his braine
    And takes the soveraigne cure
  Of the fraile Microcosme, an empire
  Which oft commotions doe distemper.

For Will, seduc'd by carnall Appetite,
    Her dictates doth despise.
Thus her prerogative shee looseth quite
    And her high dignityes.
  But divine Grace can Her alone
  Restore unto the regall Throne.

By whose assistance Man acquireth power
    Unto an higher pitch to clime;
And to become a glorious Conquerour
    Over both Death and Time.
  Thus Hee, who was a Zoophyte
  At first, becomes an Angell bright.

Ibid.

UNCONSTANCYE

SOMETIMES I am transfigur'd to a saint,
    And seeme like those who mett upon Mount Tabor;
    And then againe My Soule, through feare wax'd faint,
Doth in the Valley of Gehennor labour.
      Sometimes I mount like fire, or aire;
      Then, petrify'd by cold dispaire,
        I to the center sinke,
          And my self thinke
          At the pitte's brinke.

Lord, ballance mee with discreete moderation,
But from my heeles the clogges of Sinne untye,
Least that I fall too low, through desperation,
Nor through presumption let mee soare too high.
      But let thy Grace teach mee to acte,
      And to observe a middle tract.
        Hee that on waxen plumes
          To rise presumes,
          Himself consumes.

Ibid.

THE BURTHEN

WHILE on my self I doe reflect,
    I spy a brittle House of clay,
    With many imperfections deck't,
Which, while I labour to correct,
To these I new additions lay.
So fraile, so vaine am I in each respect,
    Oh God, teach mee thy way.

Knevet   I beare a Burthen on my backe,
And lay it downe to lessen it,
Bicause it makes my shoulders cracke;
But I so much discretion lacke,
Am so devoyde of sense, and witt,
That I more weight still on the same doe packe.
    Oh God, my Sinne remitt.

Thou dost, oh Lord, poore Soules invite,
That are surcharg'd with burthens great,
To seeke for succour from thy might,
Who wilt their heavy loades make light.
My Soule doth, therefore, Thee intreate
That Thou would'st please to ease me of my weight.
    Lord, doe mee not forgett.

Ibid.

LATHUM

WILLIAM LATHUM (*fl.* 1634). Nothing is known of the life
of this interesting poet. He may have been a student of
Emmanuel College, Cambridge. Author of a volume of
verses *Phyala Lachrymarum...Together with sundry choyce
Meditations of Mortalitie,* 1634. The poems are Elizabethan in
matter and style. The "Elegy" is full of good passages and is
interesting historically since it mourns the death of a Cambridge scholar and was probably written by another Cambridge
student only four years before the appearance of *Lycidas.* The
Meditations are often excellent and the one entitled "Pro-
sopopeia..." is one of the best things in this anthology.

PROSOPOPEIA CORPORIS ANIMAE VALEDICTURI:
ADIOS A RIVEDERCI

M Y lovely frend, that long hast been content
    To dwell with mee in my poore Tenement,
    Whose bulke and all the stuffe, both warp and woofe,
Is all of clay, the floor and the roofe:
Though yet thou ne're foundst fault; ne didst upbraid
This homely hermitage, so meanly made;
O mine owne darling, my deere daintie one,
And wilt thou now indeed from me be gone?
Ah, for thou seest all running to decay,
The thatchie covering's now nigh falne away:
The windows, which give light to every roome,
Broken, and dimme, and mistie beene become.
The Mill-house and selfe Miller's out of frame,
My Kitchen smoakes, my larder is to blame;
And from the Studds each where the home doth shrink,
And the breeme cold blowes in at every chinke,
The brases and supporters of my house
Tremble, and waxen wondrous ruinous.

Lathum   So that all bee it grieve me to the heart,
              To thinke that thou and I (old friends) must part;
              Yet, sith my Cabban's all out of repaire,
              (Darling) farewell, goe sojourne now else where,
              In some cleane place, untill that premier Main
              That built mee first, rebuild mee up againe
              All of the selfe same stuffe, but with such art,
              So polisht, and imbellisht every part,
              That it shall ne're be out of Kilture more:
              Then shalt thou come againe, as heretofore,
              And dwell with mee for ever and for aye:
              So God us both blesse untill that happie day.

*Phyala Lachrymarum, or a Few
Friendly Teares...,* 1634

FELICE CHI PUO

BLEST mote he ever bee, who ever can
    Compose the joyes and sorrows of his mind,
    Chuse truth from errour, flow'r from the bran;
Willing, obey God's sacred Lawes in kinde;
Decline the vice to which hee's most inclin'd;
Richly contented bee, what ere God send;
Slight injuries, as chaffe before the winde;
Finde a fit wife, and faithfull bosome frend:
Who some, nay one, but all these things who can,
Is sure a three-fold blessed, tenfold happy man.

Ibid.

SONNET   *Lathum*

MONOCCHIO, NON E MISERO NEL PRESENZA
DEL CIECO

WHEN I consult the sacred Histories,
    And other stories of inferior sort,
    And finde therein what under mysteries,
And plainly what they of man's life report;
Oft in the prime, oft suddenly cut short,
And every day sad samples thereof see,
Mee seemes they secretly do mee exhort
To fit my selfe the very next to be,
And meekly more my misery to beare,
Compar'd with others greater in degree,
As hee, whose one eye perled is, and bleare,
Seemes blest to him who can at all not see.
    So they, who others' greater griefe and mone
    Can call to minde, gaine strength to beare their owne.

Ibid.

DOPO IL GIVOCO, COSI VA NEL SACCO IL RE,
COME IL PEDONE

IF in my weake conceit, (for selfe disport),
    The world I sample to a Tennis-court,
    Where fate and fortune daily meet to play,
I doe conceive, I doe not much misse-say.
    All manner chance are Rackets, wherewithall
They bandie men like balls, from wall to wall;
Some over Lyne, to honour and great place,
Some under Lyne, to infame and disgrace;
Some with a cutting stroke they nimbly send
Into the hazzard placed at the end;

⟨ 143 ⟩

Resembling well the rest which all they have,
Whom death hath seiz'd, and placed in their grave:
Some o're the wall they bandie quite away,
Who never more are seene to come in play:
Which intimates that even the very best
Are soone forgot of all, if once deceast.

    So, (whether silke-quilt ball it bee, or whether
Made of course cloth, or of most homely lether);
They all alike are banded to and fro,
And all at last to selfe same end do goe,
Where is no difference, or strife for place,
No odds between a Trype-wife and your Grace:
The penny-counter's every whit as good
As that which in the place of thousands stood.
When once the Audit's full cast up and made,
The learned Arts well as the manual Trade,
The Prisoner and the Judge upon the Bench,
The pampred Lady and the Kitchin wench,
The noble Lord, or Counsailor of State,
The botchy-Lazer, begging at the gate,
Like Shrubs' and Ceadars' mingled ashes, lye
Without distinction, when they once do dye.
Ah for unpartiall death, and th'homely grave
Looke equall on the free man and the slave.

    So most unpartiall umpires are these twain,
A King with them's but as a Common Swain.
No upper hand, 'twixt dust of poore and rich,
No Marshall there to sentence which is which;
And once resolv'd to powder, none can ken
The dust of Kings from dust of other men:
But as at Chesse, when once the game is doon,
The side which lost, and that as well which
    wonn,

The victor King, and conquer'd pawne, together   *Lathum*
Jumbled, are tumbled to th'same bagge of lether
Without regard whether the pawne or King
Therein lye uppermost, or underling.
   Nathelesse all sorts, each sexe of purpose winke,
And of this destinie doon seldome thinke,
Living, (alacke), as life should never faile,
And deeme of death but as an old wives' tale.

Ibid.

O VALENTE HUOMO CHI PUO ESSER MISERO

FULL easie is for men in miserie,
   Weary of life, t'importune death to die,
   Who dare not look misfortune in the face,
Nor griefe, nor paine, nor sicknesse, nor disgrace,
But cowardly with horror and dismay,
Out of themselves, oft times do runne away:
Like Grashoppers, that skip, and sing, and dance
While Summer lasts, but as flyes, in a trance
When Winter comes, with storms accompan'ed,
In every hole and corner them doe hide,
Quite out of love with life; for such to call
For death, no fortitude is at all.
   But he whose countenance at all assayes,
Is ever one, in Sun or cloudie dayes;
Whose minde can bend, as buxom as a twigge,
To all estates, bee't high, low, small or bigge,
If fortune say he must doe thus or thus,
With her the matter he doth ne're discusse;
Who with same freenesse that he wins can lose,
Who with small noise can beare all fortune's
    blowes,

Lathum

And any part that fortune shall her please
To put him to, can personate with ease;
This is a man, one of a thousand men,
A right-bred chicken of the milke-white hen.
Right truly wise and valiant is this man,
Who selfe submit to all manner weather can;
Who 'gainst it comes, for fortune doth provide,
Not mov'd with Ebbe, nor flowing of her tyde:
So great the strength of his true tempred minde
To welcome faire and foule in selfe same kinde.
   Come good? why well, and good; come bad?
     why well:
So 'gainst all paines his patience is his spell:
Hee eekes nor aggravates his weal or woe,
Ne takes long farewells of them when they goe;
And in his open door still readie stands,
When ere they come, to take them by the hands,
So evenly he knowes to beare himselfe;
Hee rich in povertie, and poore in wealth,
Either or neither can contented bee.
Oh blessed man, how free in bonds is hee,
Who though his bread too sow'r of leaven taste,
Can eate and it digest as finest paste,
And water drinke, yea vineger for need?
This is the truely valiant man indeed.

Ibid.

FROM PHYALA LACHRYMARUM   *Lathum*

1

BRING some of those Arabian merchandise,
Sweete Aromaticke Gummes, and pretious spice,
Pure Frankincense, and pounded Cynamon
Nutmegs, with Cloves, and Mace, and Saffron some,
Add Storax-Calamite, and Bengewine,
And pretious Spicknard unto these conjoyne,
Aloes, with Myrrhe, and Cassia-Fistula,
The fragrant fuell, and the spicie spray
Whereof that bird (of selfe dust, selfe worme) bred,
Doth build her neast to serve for her death-bed,
Which flaming round about her, she sits downe,
And with sweet martyrdome her selfe doth crowne.

2

Bring bashfull Pinkes in which is to discry
Sweet Embleme of faire-maiden-modestie;
Which (though of flowers least almost) the field
For sweetnesse to the greatest need not yeeld.
Then Gilliflowers, and sparkling Sops in wine,
With Rosemary and senting Eglantine,
Whose leaves (with prickles fenc'd) teach sweetest gaines
Is that that's conquer'd with the hardest paines.
    Next Hyacynths, and black-fac'd Violets,
    In which, me seemes, the God of nature sets
The world to schoole, not ever to esteeme
Ought at first sight, as it doth outwarde seeme;
But on the hidden vertue to reflect
For th'inward good, mean outsides to respect;
Sith, though this flowre be blacke, of stature low,
A hanging-guilty look, that makes no show,

⟨ 147 ⟩   10-2

Lathum   Yet amongst all scarce one may parallel
Her savory sent, and sweet delightful smell.
Bring Heart's-ease store, oh flower most blest of all,
Which all they weare, whom nothing can befall
Beyond their expectation, ill ne ought
So good, as to excesse, to tempt their thought.
Of prettie Pansies plentie let be brought,
For this flower's name doth signifie a thought;
And therefore chiefly unto such belongs
Who dare not trust their love unto their tongues:
But in a labyrinth of thoughts doe walke,
And to themselves in pleasing silence talke;
Unthinking still whatever the first thought,
So nought by them is into practice brought.
 Bring Medway Cowslips, and deft Daffodilies,
The country Primrose, and all sorts of Lillies,
And Floure-de-Luce (Le fleur de lice, more right),
Deliciae flos, the flower of delight.
 Then usher in th'obsequious Marigold;
Whose riddle who so wise is to unfold,
Why the Sun's course it daily follows so
That as that to the South or West doth goe,
So broad or narrow this doth shut or ope,
And hight for thee the faithfull Heliotrope.
Then with Rose-buds, (if Rosebuds may be found),
It tissue thicke, and traile it all around.
And last, a traile of winding Ivie let
Run all along, on either side beset
With spring of Daphnis, stain'd with drops of gold,
And Olive leaves that still with peace doth hold;
In signe that hee with conquest dy'd in peace,
And doth the number of the Saints increase
In eviternall peace.

Now forward set, in order, two and two,
And to the Temple doe before him goe,
Some with long Rosemary-branches in your hands,
Dangling with blacke, and ashie-pale Ribbands;
And some again with both your handfulls come
Of sav'ry Dyll, and senting Marjorum,
And that Thessalian herbe, whence busie bees
Suck hunny, and with waxe doe load their knees:
And all the way with slips of wormwood dresse
In signe of this dayes bitter heavinesse.
  Clean-purging Isop bring, and Germander,
With Cotton, and her sister Lavander;
Bring Balme, that quickly leales any greene wund;
And Sage that all the vitall parts keeps sound;
And Camomel, (how ever meane and base)
The Embleme of true constancie and grace;
And doth against all scornfull feet oppose,
And much more sweet for thee, and thicker, growes.
And Sallet-budded Broom, wholsome and good
To purge and eeke the waterish-wasted blood.
Bring Strawberry, Primrose, Plantan leaves, Toutsain,
And all what ever Simples, soveraigne
For man's reliefe, (for in, or outward cure)
Bring some of all, leave none behinde, be sure:
Bring Saint John's Wort, whose vertuous oyle may dare
(For skill in healing), with selfe Balme compare,
And Lungwort.

Ibid.

LEIGH

RICHARD LEIGH (1649, alive in 1675). Dramatist and poet. He achieved notoriety by attacking Dryden on the use of the Rota in *The Conquest of Granada.* His only book of verses was *Poems, upon Several Occasions, and to several Persons,* 1675.

THE ECHO

WHERE do these Voices stray
Which lose in Woods their
Way?
Erring each Step anew,
While they false Paths pursue.
Through many windings led,
Some crookedly proceed:
Some to the Ear turn back
Asking which way to take,
Wandring without a Guide
They holloa from each side,
And call and answer all
To one another's Call.

Whence may these Sounds proceed,
From Woods, or from the Dead?
Sure, Souls here once forlorn,
The Living make their Scorn.
And Shepherds that liv'd here,
Now ceasing to appear,
Mock thus in sport the Fair
That wuld not grant their Pray'r;
While Nymphs their Voices learn
And mock them in Return:

Or if at least the Sound   *Leigh*
Does from the Woods rebound,
The Woods of them complain
Who Shepherds' Vows disdain.
Woods and Rocks answer all
To the wronged Lover's Call,
How deaf soe'ere and hard,
They their Complaints regard;
Which Nymphs with Scorn repay,
More deaf, more hard, than they.

Poems, 1675

ON A PICTURE OF SNOW, AND ICE

So in those climes, fruitful in nought but Cold,
Where Nature looks with Hoary Winters old;
High Rocks, dissembling their hid Horrour, smile,
Top't thus with Snow which does their Crags beguile;
A like Hand here the Earth's white Bosome spreads,
And dip't in Snow the Winter gently sheds;
As the resembling Level seemes to vie
With Clouds of unborn flakes, within the Skie;
While Mountain-tops and raised Heights all show
White, as the native High-Lands of the Snow;
The Heaven, big and teeming with white Show'rs,
Mock't by the Earth into whose lap it pow'rs.
But what does most of all this Art surprize,
One Hand drops Snow so soft and hardens Ice.

Ibid.

SEEING HER IN A BALCONE

T HE Sun at his first Rising so
    Gilding some Mountain-top, does show
    Illuminating all below.

As She does from on high appear,
And with like Glory crowns her Sphere,
Enlighteing her Horizon here.

Above those darkning Shadows plac't,
Which lower House-tops round us cast,
That usher Night, e're Day be past.

The proper Seat and only Scene
Of all things fair and all serene,
Which nearest Heaven still are seen.

Our winged Thoughts in their bold flight
Out-fly not yet our raised Sight,
Nor ever soar a braver Height.

Upwards our Eyes can nought pursue
Beyond what we now boast in view,
While we look up to Heav'n and You.

Vouchsafe then (fair One) to allow
That we, whom Fate has plac'd below,
To our Divinity may bow.

And though beneath your feet we bend,
Permit our Eyes but to ascend;
Further, our Hopes dare not pretend.

Ibid.

HERE first the Day does break,
And for Access does seek,
Repairing for Supplies
To her new-op'ned Eyes;
Then, (with a gentle Light
Gilding the Shades of Night),
Their Curtains drawn, does come
To draw those of her Room;
Both open, a small Ray
Does spread abroad the Day,
Which peepe into each Nest
Where neighb'ring Birds do rest;
Who, spread upon their yong,
Begin their Morning-Song,
And from their little home
Nearer her Window come,
While from low Boughs they hop
And perch upon the Top;
And so from Bough to Bough
Still singing, as they go,
In praise of Light and Her
Whom they to Light prefer;
By whose Protection blest,
So quietly they rest,
Secure as in the Wood
In such a Neighbourhood:
While undisturb'd they sit
Fearing no Hawk nor Net,
And here the first News sing
Of the approaching Spring:

The Spring which ever here
Does first of all appear;
Its fair Course still begun
By Her and by the Sun.   *Ibid.*

SLEEPING ON HER COUCH

THUS lovely, Sleep did first appear,
  E're yet it was with Death ally'd;
  When the first fair one like her here,
Lay down and for a little dy'd.

E're happy Souls knew how to dye,
And trod the rougher Paths to Bliss,
Transported in an Extasie,
They breath'd out such smooth waies as this.

Her Hand bears gently up her Head,
And, like a Pillow, rais'd does keep,
But, softer than her Couch, is spread,
Though that be softer then her Sleep.

Alas! that death-like Sleep or Night
Should power have to close those Eyes,
Which once vy'd with the fairest Light,
Or what gay Colours thence did rise.

Ah! that lost Beams thus long have shin'd
To them with darkness over-spread,
Unseen, as Day breaks, to the Blind,
Or the Sun rises, to the Dead.

That Sun in all his Eastern Pride
Did never see a shape so rare,
Nor Night, within its black Arms hide
A silent Beauty, half so fair.   *Ibid.*

LLUELYN

MARTIN LLUELYN (1616–1682). One of a group of "literary wits" of Christ Church, Oxford. During the Commonwealth he practised as a physician. At the Restoration he became Principal of St Mary Hall, Oxford. Then he was physician at High Wycombe, where he was afterwards Mayor. He contributed verse to many collections. His chief book of poems was *Men-Miracles, with other Poems*, 1646. It was reprinted three times during his life.

SONG

COCK-THROWING

COCKE a doodle-doe! 'tis the
    bravest game,
    Take a Cocke from his Dame,
And bind him to a stake:
How he struts! How he throwes!
How he swaggers! How he crowes!
As if the Day newly brake.
How his Mistris cackles
Thus to find him in shackles
And tyed to a Packe-thread Garter!
Oh! the Beares and the Bulls
Are but Corpulent Gulls
To the Valiant Shrove-Tide Martyr.

Men-Miracles, with other Poems, 1646

EPITHALAMIUM

TO MISTRIS M. A.

RISE from your Virgin sheets, that be
  Fy on them! a meere Nunnery.
  Who solitary Winters leads,
Turnes Bracelets to Religious Beads.
The Virgin that at Hymen stickes,
Should sell her Gemmes for th' Crucifix,
For she's a Nun the Sages tell,
That lies alone though in no Cell.
She midst her Liberties confin'd,
Her Bodie's cloister to her mind.
Be they immur'd whose lookes are wore
Pale as the Relickes they adore.
Where cheekes the Rose and Lilly paint
A Bride groome is the onely Saint.

Ibid.

MASTER

THOMAS MASTER (or MASTERS) (1603–1643). Oxford scholar and divine. Like Martin Lluelyn, a member of William Cartwright's group of "literary wits". Antony à Wood testifies that he was "esteemed a vast scholar, a general artist and linguist, a noted poet and a most florid preacher". No collection of verse stands to his name but it is known that he wrote several poems in English, Latin and Greek, one in English and Latin on the game of shovel-board, and one in Greek on the Passion. The one here (from MS.) is witty and full of sly fun.

ON LUTESTRINGS CATT-EATEN

ARE these the strings that poets feigne
    Have clear'd the Ayre, and calm'd the mayne?
    Charm'd wolves, and from the mountaine creasts
Made forests dance with all their beasts?
Could these neglected shreads you see
Inspire a Lute of Ivorie
And make it speake? Oh! think then what
Hath beene committed by my catt,
Who, in the silence of this night
Hath gnawne these cords, and marr'd them quite;
Leaving such reliques as may be
For fretts, not for my lute, but me.
Pusse, I will curse thee; may'st thou dwell
With some dry Hermit in a cell
Where Ratt neere peep'd, where mouse neere fedd,
And flyes goe supperlesse to bedd;
Or with some close-par'd Brother, where
Thou'lt fast each Saboath in the yeare;
Or else, prophane, be hang'd on Munday,
For butchering a mouse on Sunday;

Master　　　　　　Or May'st thou tumble from some tower,
And misse to light upon all fower,
Taking a fall that may untie
Eight of nine lives, and let them flye;
Or may the midnight embers sindge
Thy daintie coate, or Jane beswinge
Thy hide, when she shall take thee biting
Her cheese clouts, or her house beshiting.
What, was there neere a ratt nor mouse,
Nor Buttery ope? nought in the house
But harmelesse Lutestrings could suffice
Thy paunch, and draw thy glaring eyes?
Did not thy conscious stomach finde
Nature prophan'd, that kind with kind
Should stanch his hunger? thinke on that,
Thou caniball, and Cyclops catt.
For know, thou wretch, that every string
Is a catt-gutt, which art doth spinne
Into a thread; and how suppose
Dunstan, that snuff'd the divell's nose,
Should bid these strings revive, as once
He did the calfe, from naked bones;
Or I, to plague thee for thy sinne,
Should draw a circle, and beginne
To conjure, for I am, look to't,
An Oxford scholler, and can doo't.
Then with three setts of mapps and mowes,
Seaven of odd words, and motley showes,
A thousand tricks, that may be taken
From Faustus, Lambe, or Fryar Bacon:
I should beginne to call my strings
My catlings, and my mynikins;
And they recalled, straight should fall

To mew, to purr, to catterwaule   *Master*
From puss's belly. Sure as death,
Pusse should be an Engastranith;
Pusse should be sent for to the king
For a strange bird, or some rare thing.
Pusse should be sought to farre and neere,
As she some cunning woman were.
Pusse should be carried up and downe,
From shire to shire, from Towne to Towne,
Like to the camell, Leane as Hagg,
The Elephant, or Apish negg,
For a strange sight; pusse should be sung
In Lousy Ballads, midst the Throng
At markets, with as good a grace
As Agincourt, or Chevy-chase.
The Troy-sprung Brittan would forgoe
His pedigree he chaunteth soe,
And singe that Merlin—long deceast—
Returned is in a nyne-liv'd beast.
    Thus, pusse, thou seest what might betyde thee;
But I forbeare to hurt or chide thee;
For may be pusse was melancholy
And so to make her blythe and jolly,
Finding these strings, shee'ld have a fitt
Of mirth; nay, pusse, if that were it,
Thus I revenge mee, that as thou
Hast played on them, I've plaid on you;
And as thy touch was nothing fine,
Soe I've but scratch'd these notes of mine.

Brit. Mus. MSS., Harley MS. 6917

NORRIS

JOHN NORRIS (1657–1711). Fellow of All Souls, a High Churchman and Platonist, and the chief disciple of Male-branche in England. Finally rector in Somersetshire and recluse. Author of translations, disputations, tracts, miscellanies and poems. In 1684 appeared *Poems and Discoveries*, etc. and in 1687 *A Collection of Miscellanies*, etc.

THE MEDITATION

IT must be done, my soul, but 'tis a strange
 A dismal and mysterious change,
 When thou shalt leave this tenement of clay,
And to an unknown somewhere wing away;
When Time shall be Eternity, and thou
Shalt be thou know'st not what, and live thou
 know'st not how.

Amazing state! No wonder that we dread
 To think of Death, or view the dead.
Thou'rt all wrapt up in clouds, as if to thee
Our very knowledge had antipathy.
Death could not a more sad retinue find,
Sickness and Pain before, and Darkness all
 behind.

Some courteous ghost, tell this great secrecy,
 What 'tis you are, and we must be.
You warn us of approaching death, and why
May we not know from you what 'tis to dye?
But you, having shot the gulph, delight to see
Succeeding souls plunge in with like uncertainty.

When Life's close knot by writ from Destiny,   *Norris*
        Disease shall cut, or Age unty;
When after some delays, some dying strife,
The soul stands shiv'ring on the ridge of life;
With what a dreadful curiosity
Does she launch out into the sea of vast Eternity!

So when the spacious globe was delug'd o'er,
        And lower holds could save no more,
On th'utmost bough th'astonish'd sinners stood,
And view'd th'advances of th'encroaching flood.
O'er topp'd at length by th'element's encrease,
With horrour they resign'd to the untry'd abyss.

A Collection of Miscellanies, etc. 1687

THE CHOICE

Stet quicunque volet potens
Aulae culmine lubrico etc.

SENECA, *Thyestes*, I. 391

No! I shan't envy him, who'er he be
        That stands upon the battlements of state;
        Stand there who will for me,
        I'd rather be secure than great.
Of being so high the pleasure is but small
But long the ruin, if I chance to fall.

Let me in some sweet shade serenely lye,
Happy in leisure and obscurity;
        Whilst others place their joys
        In popularity and noise.
Let my soft minutes glide obscurely on,
Like subterraneous streams, unheard, unknown.

Norris
Thus when my days are all in silence past
A good plain country-man I'll dye at last.
Death cannot chuse but be
To him a mighty misery
Who to the world was popularly known
And dies a stranger to himself alone.

Ibid.

MY ESTATE

How do I pity that proud wealthy clown,
That does with scorn on my low state look
down!
Thy vain contempt dull earth-worm cease,
I won't for refuge fly to this
That none of Fortune's blessings can
Add any value to the man.
This all the wise acknowledge to be true;
But know I am as rich, more rich than you.

While you a spot of Earth possess with care
Below the notice of the Geographer,
I by the freedom of my soul,
Possess, nay more, enjoy the whole:
To th'Universe a claim I lay;
Your writings shew, perhaps you'll say;
That's your dull way; my title runs more high;
'Tis by the charter of Philosophy.

From that a firmer title I derive
Than all your courts of Law doth ever give.
A title that more firm doth stand
Than does even your very land

And yet so generous and free
    That none will e'er bethink it me,
Since my possessions tend to no man's loss,
I all enjoy, yet nothing I ingross.

Throughout the works divine I cast my eye,
Admire their beauty and their harmony.
    I view the glorious host above
    And Him that made them praise and love.
    The flowery meads and fields beneath
    Delight me with their odorous breath.
Thus is my joy by you not understood,
Like that of God when He said all was good.

Nay! what you'd think less likely to be true,—
I can enjoy what's yours much more than you.
    Your meadow's beauty, I survey
    Which you prize only for its hay.
    There can I sit beneath a tree
    And write an ode or elegy.
What to you care does to me pleasure bring,
You own the cage, I in it sit and sing.

Ibid.

SEEING A GREAT PERSON LYING IN STATE

WELL, now I needs must own
    That I hate greatness more and more;
    'Tis now a just abhorence grown
What was antipathy before;
    With other ills I could dispence,
    And acquiesce in providence.
    But let not Heaven my patience try
With this one plague, lest I repine and dye.

I knew indeed before
That 'twas the great man's wretched fate
While with the living to endure
The vain impertinence of State.
But sure, thought I, in death he'll be
From that and other troubles free:
What e'er his life, he then will lye
As free, as undisturb'd, as calm as I.

But 'twas a gross mistake.
Honour, that too officious ill,
Won't even his breathless corps forsake
But haunts and waits about him still.
Strange persecution, when the grave
Can't the distressed martyr save!
What remedy can there avail
Where Death the great catholicon does fail?

Thanks to my stars that I
Am with so low a fortune blest,
That whate're blessings Fate deny
I'm sure of privacy and rest.
'Tis well; thus lone I am content
And rest as in my element.
Then Fate, if you'll appear my friend,
Force me not 'gainst my nature to ascend.

No, I would still be low,
Or else I would be very high,
Beyond the state which mortals know,
A kind of semi-deity.
So of the regions of the air
The highest and the lowest quiet are,
But 'tis this middle height I fear
For storms and thunder are ingendr'd there.   *Ibid.*

PICK

SAMUEL PICK (*fl.* 1639). Nothing is known of this poet. His only book was *Festum Voluptatis, or the Banquet of Pleasure,* . . . *Containing divers choyce Love-Poesies, Songs, Sonnets, Odes, Madrigalls, Satyrs, Epigrams, Epitaphs and Elegies,* 1639.

SONNET

TO HIS MISTRESSE CONFIN'D

O THINKE not Phoebe 'cause a cloud
    Doth now thy silver brightnesse shrowde,
        My wandring eyes
Can stoope to common beauties of the skies.
Rather be kind, and this eclipse
Shall neither hinder eye nor lippes,
        For we shall meet
Within our hearts and kisse when none shall
    see't.

Nor canst thou in the prison be
Without some loving signe of me:
        When thou dost spie
A sunne beame peepe into the roome, 'tis I;
For I am hid within that flame,
And thus into the chamber came,
        To let thee see
In what a martyrdome I burne for thee.

When thou doest touch the Lute, thou maist
Thinke on my heart, on which thou playest;
        When each sad tone
Upon the strings doth shew my deeper groane;

Pick   When thou dost please they shall rebound,
With nimble aire strucke to the sound,
       Of thine own voice:
O thinke how much I tremble, and rejoyce.

There's no sad picture that doth dwell
Upon thy arras wall, but well
       Resembles me.
No matter though our age doth not agree,
Love can make old as well as time,
And he that doth but twenty chyme,
       If he dare prove
As true as I, shewes fourscore yeares in Love.

Festum Voluptatis, 1639

AN ELEGIE UPON THE DEATH OF HIS DEARE FRIEND, MISTRESSE PRISCILLA WADL

HERE though her spot-lesse, span-long life be spent,
Are silent steps to shew where goodnesse went.
Nature did in such rare compleatnesse make her,
To shew her Art, and so away did take her.
For she was onely to us wretches lent
For a short time to be our president.
Goods we inherit daily, and possession:
O, that in goodnesse were the same succession!
For then before her soul to heaven she breath'd,
She had to each of us a part bequeath'd
Of her true wealth; and closing thus her eyes,
Would have enrich'd her sex with legacies.

Ibid.

PORDAGE

SAMUEL PORDAGE (1633–1691?). Son of John Pordage, the astrologer and mystic of Bradfield in Berkshire. Studied law and medicine. Dramatist, poet, satirist and translator. His poetic works were *Poems upon Several Occasions*, 1660; *Mundorum Explicatio*, 1661; *Azaria and Hushai*, 1682 (an heroical poem in answer to Dryden's *Absalom and Achitophel*); and *The Medal revers'd, etc.* 1682 (in answer to Dryden's poem *The Medal*). He wrote a vigorous couplet. He is "Lame Mephibosheth, the wizard's son" in the second part of *Absalom and Achitophel*. His Cavalier verses in lyrical measures are good.

TO HIS MISTRESS

As Phoebus doth excel the Moon's dim light,
  Or as the Moon excells the dullest Star,
  Her Beauty and Complexion in my sight
  Excell all others' I have seen so far:
Her Sun-like beams of beauty shine so bright,
  That others in her sight Eclipsed are:
The fairest faces are but foiles; each one
Wears but a borrow'd lustre from her Sun.

Her Shape in Wax it were most hard to frame,
  Nor Painters to expresse their rarest Skill
Could ever counterfeit so neer the same,
  But blemish theirs her better Beauty will;
Though Venus, who for Beauty had the Name,
  Compare with her should, she'd be fairest still;
Paris gave her the Ball as Beauties' Queen,
But she had miss'd it had he mine but seen.

Her Aubourn hair in Crisped Curles doe dangle
  Upon her Ivory shoulders, when it spreads
Sly nets, where hearts themselves doe soon intangle
  And captive lye, enchain'd by those bright threads,

Spreading soft chaines and snares in every angle,
       It takes all Hearts whose eye those mazes treads:
Hearts here imprison'd—never can get out—
Those soft Meandres wander must about!

Her Ivory-pollish'd Front with seemly cheere,
       Grac'd at the bottom with a double bow,
Where all the Graces in their Throne appeare,
       Where Love and awfull Majesty doe grow,
Expands it self, and shows a feild more clear
       Than Candid Lilys, or the virgin snow;
Her Eyes like Suns shoot rayes more sharp than Darts,
Which wound all Flinty, Love-despising Hearts.

Those twinkling Stars, those sparkling Diamond-stones,
       Those glorious Suns, where dwells the Eastern Light;
Pierce, with the vigor of their Charmes, the bones
       Of daring Him, who gains of them a sight;
Beholding Kills, yet he their losse bemoanes,
       And'd rather die than, they shut, live in Night.
Her Nose, a comely Prominence, doth part
Her Cheeks, the mirror of Dame Nature's Art.

Her Cheeks are damask Roses blown in June,
       Being equally with Virgin Lilys mixt;
Or snowy milk with blushing Strawb'ries strewn,
       Where equal strife the red and white's betwixt;
Or pure vermillion, on white Sattin shewn,
       By Painter's rarest Skill and pencil fixt:
Those Cheeks no Colour's liveliest dye can paint,
Scarlet and snow seem, to their true ones, faint.

Her lipps are snips of Scarlet Gilliflowers,
       Spread with the tincture of Vermillion hew,
Bless'd in Self-kisses, past our humane powers
       To touch. So high a bliss what Mortal knew?

⟨ 168 ⟩

Between those rubie Gates slide spicy showers,   *Pordage*
        Which those slain by her eyes with life imbue:
Angellick sounds and charming smiles so nice
Thence flow, which make her presence Paradice.

Within the portal of her Mouth's lock'd fast
        (Which, when she sings, she is enforc'd to show),
The Orient's Treasure in due order plac'd,
        Of more than precious pearles a double row;
Which stand in Sea-born Coral borders chaste,
        Like Crimson Sattin purl'd with silver snow.
Her smooth and dimpl'd Chin doth under lye,
Where Envy's self cannot a fault espie.

Her Neck's a gracefull Tower of spotlesse snow,
        An Alabaster prop to that fair head,
Where Witt, Arts, Wisdome, in perfection grow;
        Its basis where are beauties also spread:
For azure streames through milky feilds do flow,
        Where blew with white like Heav'n is married:
Her breasts like lilly'd Globes or Mounts appear,
Whose summits Crown'd with Crimson cheries are.

Her Arms due measure of proportion have,
        Her hands the types of snowy Excellence
With Onyx tipp'd; her legs and feet enslave
        Our eyes, and Captive hold from falling thence.
Her whole frame's equal Symetry is brave,
        And to spectators pays a recompence:
Argus himself cannot discern the rest,
But I presume the hidden beauties best.

                        Poems upon Several Occasions, 1660

〈 169 〉

TO LYDIA

BEING RETIRED PRIVATELY INTO THE COUNTRY

Now to the secret Groves is Lydia gone
Stoll'n from us all, meaning to live alone
Among the silent woods, where she may be
From busie servants' entertainments free;
And hear the pleasant songsters of the Groves
With whistling layes resound their growing Loves;
With uncontrouling freedom view the trammells
Of Flora, which the fragrant meads inammels;
With pleasure walke and see the crystall brooks,
Catching the sportive fish with silver hooks.
Conversing with the flowry Napaeae;
Making diversity of flow'rs agree
Bound up together; 'mong the shady trees
Daunce in a Circle with the Dryades;
Feeding on cleanly, though but homely food;
Esteem'd the only Goddess of the wood.
O how I fear those rural pleasures may
Entice her there to make a tedious stay:
But I with vows will Frosty Hyems move
To hast the ruines of the leavy grove:
Pray cold-mouth Boreas kiss her tender cheek
To make her shelter in the town to seek,
Where conversation and warm fires do bring
Though frost without doors lies, within, a spring.

Ibid.

CORYDON'S COMPLAINT
Pordage

THOSE joys that us'd to flatter me
O Phyllis when I courted thee
Under yon shady beechen tree
       To cruell grief are chang'd.

Torments my pleasures, griefs my joy,
Pains my quiet rest destroy,
Since thou'rt to Corydon grown coy,
       And from my Love estrang'd.

Did e're I your commands neglect
That thus my sute you now reject
And pay my love with disrespect,
       My kindness with disdain?

Say how I purchace may reliefe,
Or murther'd must I be by grief?
Speak that my torments may be brief;
       Give death to ease my pain.

If you are pleas'd to martyr me
Or binde me unto slavery
There is another tyranny
       That you may exercise—

Those burning flames your eyes can give
A Slave, bound by Love's Chaines I live,
Nay, without hope of a reprieve;
       Thus you may tyrannize.

Since that my words are spent in vain,
Whilst Cruel you laugh at my pain,
I at the feet of your disdain
       Will fall, and prostrate lye

Pordage

Henceforth I'le banish all my pleasure,
Since you the chiefest of my Treasure,
Have heaped my Griefs beyond all Measure,
      I'le yield to destiny.

Ibid.

TO LUCIA PLAYING ON HER LUTE, ANOTHER

WHEN last I heard your nimble fingers play
    Upon your Lute, nothing so sweet as they
    Seem'd: all my soul fled ravish'd to my ear,
That sweetly animating sound to hear.
My ravish'd Heart with play kept equal time,
Fell down with you, with you did Ela climbe,
Grew sad or lighter, as the tunes you plai'd,
And with your Lute a perfect measure made:
If all, so much as I, your Musick Love,
The whole world would at your devotion move;
And, at your speaking Lute's surpassing charmes,
Embrace a lasting peace, and fling by Arms.

Ibid.

DAMON ON AMARILLIS DANCING IN A RING

SEE my fortune, see my fortune,
      How she flyes me
      And denys me;
Wo alas! wo alas too soon
      Still I follow!
      Still I follow!
      But she flyes me
      And denys me,
And cannot be won.

Cruel sport in this sort   *Pordage*
        With woes to fill me
        Which will kill me.
Ah! from this pain release me.
        For whilst she flyes,
        My eyes
        They discover
        I'm a lover,
And that it is her self must ease me.
        But she flys me
        And denys me;
Still I follow wrapt in woe.

She moves swiftly and yet sweetly;
        Don't forsake me,
        I'le o're take thee
If thou wilt pity bestow:
        Cruel sport,
        In this sort
        To increase my fires
        And desires
And to exhibit my despaire;
        She shifts her place,
        Apace
        I after move
        Being urg'd by Love;
But in vain still my endeavours are.

                                       Ibid.

PRESTWICH

EDMUND PRESTWICH (*fl.* 1651). Nothing is known of this poet. Author of a volume which had two editions in 1651: *Hippolitus, Translated out of Seneca: together with divers other Poems.*

HOW TO CHUSE A MISTRESS

FIRST I would have a face exactly fair,
Not long, nor yet precisely circular.
A smooth high brow, where neither Age, nor yet
A froward peevishness hath wrinckles set.
And under that a pair of clear black eyes
To be the windows of the Aedifice;
Not sunck into her head, nor starting out,
Not fix'd, nor rolling wantonly about,
But gently moving, as to whet the sight
By some fresh object, not the appetite;
Their Orbs both equal, and divided by
A wel-proportion'd nose's Ivory.
The nostrils open, fit to try what air
Would best preserve the Mansion, what impair.
The colour in her cheek so mixt, the eye
Cannot distinguish where the red doth lye,
Or white; but ev'ry part thereof, as loth
To yeeld in either, equally hath both.
The mouth but little, whence proceeds a breath,
Which might revive one in the gates of death,
And envy strike in the Panchayan groves
When their spic'd tops a gentle East-wind moves.
The lips ruddy, as blushing to be known
Kissing each other, by the Lookers on;

And these not to perpetual talk dispos'd,   *Prestwich*
Nor always in a lumpish silence clos'd;
But ev'ry word her innocence brings forth
Sweetned by a discreet and harmles mirth.
The teeth even and white; a dimpled chin;
And all these clothed with the purest skin.
Then, as good painters ever use to place
The darker shadow to the fairer face,
A sad, brown hair, whose am'rous curles may tye
The Pris'ners fast, ta'ne captive by her eye.
Thus would I have her face. And for her mind,
I'd have it cloth'd in Vertue, not behind
The other's Beauty; for a house thus drest
Should be provided of a noble guest.
Then would I have a body so refin'd
Fit to support this face, enclose this mind.
When all these Graces I in one doe prove,
Then may Death blind me if I do not love.
Yet there is one thing more must needs concur;
She must love me as well as I love her.

*Hippolitus . . . together with divers
other Poems*, 1651

PRUJEAN

THOMAS PRUJEAN (1620–1662). Son of Sir Francis Prujean, the famous surgeon of Charles II. Studied medicine and became a Fellow of the College of Physicians. He published two books of verse while he was a student at Cambridge. They were *Aurorata* and *Love's Looking-Glasse, Divine and Humane.* Both appeared in 1644 and may have been issued together.

A SONNET

WOUND not so deepe, unlesse you will
Send mee a balme to cure the ill,
Or breath your scorne, that I may dy
And rid mee of my misery.
'Tis better to endure that,
Then live for nought but shooting at.

I'll not repeat your being faire,
The envy of Cynthia shews you are;
Nor can my heart proclaime you lesse,
If bleeding wounds the truth express;
Yet think I doe not Gods would let
Nature the greater honour get.

The soul's the purer of the two;
Then how pure must it be in you
To keepe it so, sin not 'twill bee
Held then in th'inferioritie!
Is't not a sin to tyrannize?
Then doe not use it, and bee wise.

That blush will weare because 'tis given   *Prujean*
By earth's grand artist, not by heaven.
Nor is that gracefull stampe of white
Of more endurance. Your delight
Nature stiles equall to ours, then,
(Since you are lov'd), faith, love again.

Aurorata, 1644

RAWLET

JOHN RAWLET (1642–1686). Student of divinity who spent most of his life in the north of England. Author of several religious works which proved to be popular. *The Christian Monitor* was in its twenty-fifth edition in 1699 and was often reissued in the eighteenth century. His only book of verses was also appreciated. As *Poetick Miscellanies* it appeared in 1687 and was republished in 1691 and in the next century. There is a gentle authority about some of his poems.

AN ACCOUNT
OF MY LIFE IN THE NORTH
BENE QUI LATUIT BENE VIXIT

SINCE you, dear friend, wonder how here I live,
 This homely Verse a brief account shall give.
  I live, if not in pleasure, yet at ease,
Not in loud laughters, but in silent peace;
And though I rarely meet with merriment,
I more a stranger am to discontent.
Here's no excess, nor are things needful scant;
I seldom feast, but yet I never want.
No dainties here to luxury invite;
Our food serves well the sober appetite,
Which need not be with poignant Sawces drest,
Our healthful Hunger of all Sawce is best.
Doctors we have none, nor much need them here;
The Doctors we more than Diseases fear;
For Country-folks think they sell death too dear.
Altho' I lie not on a rich Down-bed,
Yet do sweet sleeps refresh my weary head.
No Walks or Gardens here, but yet the Field
And fragrant Meadows equal pleasures yield.

No Lutes or Viols entertain my ear,   *Rawlet*
But more melodious Birds I daily hear.
Riches I have not, nor do riches need,
Whilst here at easy rates we clothe and feed,
I have no Servants whom I may command,
Nor have I work that needs a Servant's hand.
I am not high enough to envied be,
Nor do I one whom I should envy see.
Here's no applause to make me proud or vain,
Nor do I meet with censures or disdain.
My people, if they are not wise and great,
Are not untractable through self-conceit;
No factions, giddy heads that make a Schism
For fear of Popery or Arminianism;
No sawcy, arrogant controllers, such
That cry, "This is too little, this too much;"
No such vile wretches who their Preacher hate
'Cause he reproves sin at too smart a rate;
Wherefore I envy not flocks of more wealth,
Which give more trouble while they have less
    health.
If of Companions I have no great store,
With my own mind I may converse the more;
And from my old Friends tho' I am confin'd,
Letters may keep us in each other's mind;
Or if, whilst buried here, I lose their love,
I'l fix my mind on surer things above;
But need I Friends, need I Companions crave,
Whilst I as many Friends as Neighbours have?
Or if I want the joy of bosom Friends,
I 'scape the pain which still that joy attends;
For whilst they live our hearts oft ake with fear,
But break and bleed when of their death we hear.

Rawlet And if I want the comfort of a Wife,
I have the pleasures of a single life;
If I no Gallants here, nor Beauties see,
From lavish Love and Courtship I am free.
What fine things else you in the South can name,
Our North can shew as good, if not the same;
Ev'n as in Winter you have shorter Nights,
But Summer us with longer Days requites.
Thus if my want of joy makes life less sweet,
Death then will seem less bitter when we meet.
But what is this World's Joy? 'Tis Innocence
And Virtue that do truest joys dispence;
If Innocence and Virtue with me dwell,
They'l make a Paradice of an Hermit's Cell.

Poetick Miscellanies, 1687

A PLAIN PARAPHRASE

LET who will climb to heights of Honour, where
What they with labour get, they hold with fear.
On lower ground give me an humble nest,
In private shades with peace and safety blest.
Here I'l in silence pass my sliding years,
Strange to great men, strange to their cares and fears.
In this obscure, quiet recess shall I
An honest Country Parson live and die.
But dreadful terrors do his death attend,
Who all his time in crowds and noise doth spend,
Knows not himself, nor thinks of his last end.

Ibid.

RICHARDS

NATHANIEL RICHARDS (*fl.*1630–1654). Dramatist and poet, perhaps of Kentish origin. In 1630 appeared *The Celestiall Publican, a Sacred Poem, etc.* Two years later it was reissued as *Poems, Divine, Morall and Satyricall* and in 1641 it was reprinted with additions as *Poems Sacred and Satyricall.* His play on the empress Messalina was praised by Genest.

From   MIDNIGHT'S MEDITATION

WHEN I contemplate Heav'n, and take no care
    For worldly vanities, then my soule how faire,
    How amorously faire thou art, destroying sinnes.
Man's a rich Monarch; then true joy beginnes;
Never till then. Never did any fight
'Gainst sinne but gain'd unspeakeable delight.
This, when I thinke upon, and practise too,
Heavn's in my eye: want, nor the worst of woe,
Distracts my senses. But when I roote my mind
On this rude world, Vertue is soone strooke blind.
Witt, reason, all my senses are confounded,
Devills assault my flesh, my soule is wounded.
Save me, O save me Lord, thy worthlesse Creature;
Pittie the weaknesse of my Mortall nature.
Forgive all forfeitures my sinnes have made,
Vowes, Promises, protestations never paid.
I promis'd still to mend, to turne mine eyes
From sinfull waies: yet Heav'n knowes all were lies,
Shame to my soule. How dare I then looke up,
Expect least solace from sweete Mercie's Cup?
O, I am angry, next to th'very heart;
I act not thy will, Lord, but mine owne part,

Richards   A sinfull Tragicke Part which will deface
             My soule. Helpe, Heav'n; send thy restraining Grace.
             One drop of Grace Celestiall can refresh
             A fainting soule; cleanse Lord my corrupt flesh.

                                    Poems Sacred and Satyricall, 1641

         From   MIDNIGHT'S MEDITATION

O   INFINITE sweetnesse, O Immortall love,
           Thou God the Father that dost rule above
           The Highest Heavens; Thee, in the blessed Name
Of Jesus Christ, (Theanthropos), that came
To save beleeving soules, I aske, implore,
Pardon, O, pardon; out with sinne's rotten core
Rooted too neare my heart; whisper thy feare
Into my soule; let me not onely heare
Thy sacred word but, in the practicke part,
Make perfect use of it; ne're let me start
From thee my God; let sad Teares from mine eyes
And sighes from my heart expresse my grievancies.
Though I fall foule and fearefully each day,
Lord let me not fall finally away!
        And if I needs must fall, let my fall be
        From death to life, from sinne to sanctity.

                                                      Ibid.

ROSS(E)

ALEXANDER ROSS(E) (1590–1654). Studied theology and divinity at Aberdeen. Schoolmaster, chaplain to Charles I, on the advice of Laud, and vicar of Carisbrooke, Isle of Wight. Wrote numerous books in English and Latin on theology, history and philosophy. Evelyn refers to him as "the old historian and poet" and he is mentioned in *Hudibras*. In 1637 *Poemata* appeared and in 1642 *Mel Heliconium, or Poeticall Honey, etc.* These fragments, which Mr John Drinkwater discovered, represent Rosse's only achievements that are above mediocrity.

TWO FRAGMENTS

I

WE'RE all in Atalanta's case,
　　　　We run apace
　　　Until our wandring eyes behold
　　　　The glitt'ring gold:
And then we lose in vanity
Our race, and our virginity.

II

Who glory in your golden hair,
And in smooth Alabaster skins:
And think with Swans you may compare
In whitenesse, that your cheeks and chins
　　　Can match white Lillies, and
　　　Vermillion;
　　　Yet think upon
　　　The flower that's in your hand.

Mel Heliconium, or Poeticall Honey, 1642

ROWE

ELIZABETH ROWE (*née* SINGER) (1674–1737). Daughter of a nonconformist, Somersetshire minister. In 1696 *Poems on several Occasions* was issued under the pseudonym of "Philomela". (Second edition, 1737.) Matthew Prior printed one of her pastorals with his own poems; Dr Isaac Watts commended her divine poems; Pope printed her elegy on the death of her husband at the end of the second edition of *Eloisa and Abelard.* Her poems were translated into German and proved very popular.

TO MADAM S—— AT THE COURT

COME, prethee, leave the Courts,
    And range the Fields with me;
    A thousand pretty Rural sports
        I'le here invent for thee.

Involv'd in blissful innocence
    Wee'l spend the shining day,
Untoucht with that mean influence
    The duller world obey.

About the flowry Plains wee'l rove
    As gay and unconfin'd
As are inspir'd by thee and love
    The saleys of my mind.

Now seated by a lovely Stream
    Where beauteous Mermaids haunt,
My Song, while William is my Theam,
    Shall them and thee inchant.

Then in some gentle, soft retreat,
    Secure as Venus' Groves,
We'l all the charming things repeat
    That introduc'd our loves.

⟨ 184 ⟩

I'le pluck fresh Garlands for thy brows,   *Rowe*
    Sweet as a Zephir's breath,
As fair and well-design'd as those
    The Elisyum Lovers wreath.

And, like those happy Lovers, we,
    As careless and as blest,
Shall, in each others converse, be
    Of the whole world possest.

Then prethee, Phillis, leave the Courts,
    And range the Fields with me,
Since I so many harmless sports
    Can here procure for thee.

Poems on several Occasions, 1696

SHIPMAN

THOMAS SHIPMAN (1632–1680). Friend of most Royalist poets. A Northamptonshire squire who was captain of a trained band after the Restoration. Author of a rhymed tragedy and a book of verses, *Carolina, or Loyal Poems*, which was issued posthumously in 1683.

THE SHOWER, 1653

TO MRS S. V. BEING IN THE RAIN. RAPTIM

THUS looks a Sea-Nymph when she leaves
 Her Bed, and rises from the Waves:
 Thus Flowers we in Water steep
That so they may their freshness keep:
Your Tresses are like Sol's bright Rayes
When he appears in rainy dayes.
Diana, when she did appear
I'th'Fountain, was not half so fair.

Carolina, or Loyal Poems, 1683

From   THE FROST 1654

TO MR W. L.

NATURE'S inslav'd; her very Breath confin'd,
 Her Lungs are stopt and cannot gather Wind.
 Sometimes she's raging mad, and fiercely blows,
Foaming and Froathing all the Earth with Snows.
Those downy show'rs appear, (which Boreas brings),
As though the moulting Clouds had mew'd their wings.
What else is Snow but feather'd drizzel, blown
Fro'th'Sky, where their swift Pinnions late had flown?
No other flights than these now haunt the Air,
Till lym'd with frost they're forc'd to tarry here.

The Air's so thick it does like th'Dead-Sea flow,   *Shipman*
Where Birds, with feather'd Oars, can scarcely row;
And hollow Clouds, ramm'd full as they can bear,
Discharge Hail-shot in Volleys through the Air.
Those Dew-drops that upon the Earth are found,
Right Pearls they are, and have the glitt'ring ground.
Wherever any grassy Turf is view'd,
It seems a Tansie all with Sugar strew'd.   *Ibid.*

THE KISS, 1656

TO MRS C.

HOLD not your Lips so close; dispence
Treasures, Perfumes, and Life from thence.
Squeeze not those full-ripe Cherries; this
Becomes a Simper, not a Kiss.
There's danger to lock up your Breath,
It Cousin-German is to Death.
None baggs up wind, the Merchant swears,
Unless some wrinkled Laplanders.
What needs this Guard? it is small sence
Thus to hedge in a double Fence.
Clos'd Lips express but silent Blisses,
And at the best are but dumb Kisses.
You are with Cupid little kind
To make him Dumb as well as Blind.
Such Smacks but shew a silent state;
Kisses should be articulate.
An open-mouthed Kiss speaks sence,
It is the Lover's eloquence.
Let yours speak out then! there's no Bliss
To th' Pronuntiation of a kiss.   *Ibid.*

THE OLD MAN, 1658

AN EPITAPH UPON MY GRANDFATHER, MR T. S.

HERE lies an aged Corps, which late
Incag'd a Soul, whom neither fate
Nor Times could change from its first State.

Oppressed more with Age than cares;
Respected more for Silver hairs
Than Gold; for Wisdom more than Years.

Happy in every Child he had;
Happy in self, and only sad
Being born in good days, but deceas'd in bad.

Ibid.

GRIEF, 1664

UPON THE DEATH OF MY DEAR SISTER, MRS P. S.

FAREWEL, dear Sister! precious Soul, farewel!
Go to thy fitter place, where thou wilt dwell
With thy Companions, spotless Virgins; where
Thy Veil will be as white as any there:
Of thine own spinning too, 'ere thou went'st hence,
Made up of Chastity and Innocence.
But now, alas, this sad truth I have learn'd,
None can write Elegies that are concern'd.
(Objects too near are never seen so well
As those which at remoter distance dwell).
Grief, when 'tis gotten to the highest pitch,
Damms up our tears and locks up all our Speech.

Ibid.

STEVENSON

MATTHEW STEVENSON (*fl.* 1654–1685). Poet and writer of broadsides. Member of an interesting group of literary men which included Alexander Brome, Valentine Oldys, Edward Baynard, Edward Bostocke and Henry Bold (who wrote of Stevenson's "queint facetiousness". For this see the opening lines of "An Elegy upon old Freeman"). In 1654 appeared *Occasion's Offspring, etc.*, and in 1661 *The Twelve Moneths. Poems* was issued in 1665 and another volume of miscellaneous verse under the same title in 1673.

THE JOVIALL JOURNEY

UP, Phoebus, up, and guild the horizon!
    For Love and beauty are a progress gone.
    Stand not to gaze, least thy too curious eye
A fairer Daphne in this Coach espie:
And thou great Prince of winds vouchsafe to us
The gentle gusts of sweet breath'd Zepherus.
Come, yee auspicious Choristers of the aire,
Let those faire Ladies see yee promise faire.
Cherp up, (sweet Syren of the woods), nere feare,
Here is no Tereus; come, be merry here,
And if the dust, it self too proudly reares,
Some gentle Cloud rebuke it with its teares:
Let th'Earth's green Plush, and floscular starres out vye
The brighter Orbs of the frost-warning skie;
Let every brook present some pretty toy,
And every hedge be lin'd with traveller's joy;
Grant Fates no inauspicious Hare may chance
To crosse, yea, through unlucky ignorance;
But as the morning, so the evening may
Answer the beauty of a glorious day.

Stevenson   Then, Sun, Wind, Raine, Earth and flowers conspire
A harmony, next the Celestiall Quire.
And when friends meet, be your embraces such
As lovers, that each minut's absence grutch.
Whilst all that see, admire your greeting kisse,
As if the body met the soule in blisse.

Occasion's Offspring, 1654

AT THE FLORISTS' FEAST IN NORWICH

THE SONG

Stay! O Stay! ye winged howers,
    The windes that ransack East and West
Have breath'd perfumes upon our flowers,
More fragrant than the Phoenix' nest:
Then stay! O Stay! sweet howers! that yee
May witnesse that which time nere see.

Stay a while, thou feather'd Syth-man,
    And attend the Queen of flowers;
Show thy self for once a blyth man,
    Come dispence with a few howers:
        Eelse we our selves will stay a while,
        And make our pastime, Time beguile.

This day is deignd to Flora's use;
    If yee will revell too, to-night
Wee'l presse the Grape, to lend ye juyce
    Shall make a deluge of delight:
        And when yee can't hold up your heads,
        Our garden shall afford ye beds.

Ibid.

"us'd hardly by the Committee, for lying in the Cathedral, and in Church-Porches, praying the Common-prayer by heart etc."

Here in this homely Cabinet,
 Resteth a poor old Anchoret;
 Upon the ground he laid all weathers,
Not as most men, gooslike on feathers.
For so indeed it came to pass,
The Lord of Lords his Landlord was.
He liv'd instead of wainscoat rooms,
Like the possest, among the tombs.
As by some Spirit thither led,
To be acquainted with the Dead.
Each morning from his bed so hallow'd,
He rose, took up his cross, and follow'd.
To every porch he did repair,
To vent himself in Common-prayer.
Wherein he was alone devout,
When preaching justled praying out.
In such procession, through the City,
Maugre the Devil and Committee,
He daily went; for which he fell,
Not into Jacob's, but Bridewell.

Ibid.

From   THE WILLOW GARLAND

How many Coronets of Daffodillies,
 Of purer Roses, and of Paphian Lillies,
 Wove thy false hope for her thou thought'st
thine own,
When Fate was wreathing Willows for thy Crown?

⟨ 191 ⟩

Stevenson   Unhappy faith, to trust so false a Love,
Could fast and loose thee in thy Myrtle Grove!
Those blissful shades, where every sacred bough
Offer'd it self to kisse, and Crown thy brow!
Thy tongue, alas! is lost in the surprize,
And nothing now is fluent, but thine Eyes,
From whose all-watery banks, these Willows spread
And plat a woful Willow for thy Head.

Poems, 1665

SONG

Should I sigh out my dayes in griefe,
    And as my beads count miseries,
My wound would meet with no reliefe,
    For all the balsome of mine eyes;
I'le therefore set my heart at rest,
And of bad market make the best.

Some set their hearts on winged wealth,
    Others to honour's towers aspire;
But give me freedom and my health,
    And there's the sum of my desire,
If all the world should pay me rent,
It could not add to my content.

There is no fence against our fate,
    Eve's daughters all are bound to sorrow,
Vicissitudes upon us wait,
    That laugh to-day, and lower to-morrow.
Why should we then with wrinkl'd care,
Deface what Nature made so fair?

Poems, or a Miscellany, 1673

TATHAM

JOHN TATHAM (*fl.* 1632–1664). "City poet" after John Taylor, in which capacity he produced many plays and pageants. Author of two volumes of verse, *The Fancies' Theater*, 1640 and *Ostella; or the Faction of Love and Beauty reconcil'd*, 1650. The former was re-issued in 1657 as *The Mirrour of Fancies*. He writes a fair Cavalier love-lyric.

AN EXCUSIVE LETTER MADE BY THE AUTHOR, FOR A FRIEND OF HIS TO HIS FATHER

As one who having rob'd, fearing no Law,
   Till hue and cry assaults him, and doth draw
   Perforce his body to the Gaole, where long
Enduring all extreames, at last is stung
With some remorce of conscience, doth relent
His wicked life, a reform'd penitent.
He goeth far that never back returnes;
An angry fire 'tis that ever burnes
Within the heart of man. Oh! then be pleas'd
To let your anger passe, and be appeas'd,
Though all this while my Infant yeares did stray,
And trod the path of follie's baiting way;
Though all this while I was in blindnesse led,
And all my sences unto fondnesse wed;
My unripen'd yeares had not the wit to finde
The vaine delights that still provoke the mind,
Till buying wit now at the dearest rate,
I gain'd experience through my best friend's hate:
Witnesse the daily teares I shed at last,
In true repentance for my follyes past.
Then, worthy Sir, your pardon let me crave;
Without your pardon I no life can have:

For better 'twere that life from body fled,
Than in your deepe disdaines lie buried.
Let my repentance plead for mine offence,
And my reformed life my innocence.

The Fancies' Theater, 1640

TO PHILOMEL

LEAVE, Philomel, to make thy moane!
'Tis I have cause to grieve alone:
Thy Woes had periods, mine must be
Invaded with fresh Crueltie.
The Joyes I have are such as may
Make the greene Spring a Winter's day;
Or such as, when desir'd, doe take
A course to kill. For pitty sake
Cease then thy noyse of woe, unlesse
Thou'lt grieve for my unhappinesse.

Ibid.

THE LETTER

GOE, pale-fac't Paper, to my Deare,
And whisper this into her eare:
Though I absent am, yet shee
Keeping thee, embraces mee.
Let no rude hand dare to touch thee,
Care not though a thousand grutch thee
Of that blisse which in her Hive
Thou enjoy'st till I arrive,
And be sure thou dost not flye
From the glances of her eye.

Where she goes be thou about her,   *Tatham*
Gad not thou abroad without her;
Nor let any dare to see
What's betweene my Love and thee.
Nay, and when she chance to sleepe,
Gently to her Bosome creepe,
Where, I charge thee, rest till shee
With her kisses waken thee.
Goe and prosper for a space,
Till I rob thee of thy place.

                                                    Ibid.

UPON MY NOBLE FRIEND,
RICHARD LOVELACE ESQUIRE,
HIS BEING IN HOLLAND, AN INVITATION

A SONG

COME, Adonis, come again,
        What distast could drive thee hence,
Where so much delight did reign,
        Sateing ev'n the Soul of Sense?
And though thou unkind hast prov'd,
        Never Youth was more belov'd.
            Then lov'd Adonis come away,
            For Venus brooks not thy delay.

Wert thou sated with the Spoil
        Of so many Virgins' Hearts,
And therefore didst change thy Soil,
        To seek fresh in other parts:
Dangers wait on forreigne Game,
        We have Deer more sound and tame.
            Then lov'd Adonis, etc.

Tatham

Phillis, fed with thy delights,
    In thy absence pines away;
And Love too hath lost his Rites:
    Not one Lasse keeps Holi-day.
They have chang'd their Mirth for Cares,
    And do onely sigh thy Airs.
        Then lov'd Adonis, etc.

Elpine, in whose sager looks
    Thou wert wont to take Delight,
Hath forsook his Drink and Books,
    'Cause he cann't enjoy thy sight;
He hath laid his Learning by,
    'Cause his wit wants Company.
        Then lov'd Adonis come away,
        For Friendship brooks not thy Delay.

All the Swains that once did use
    To converse with Love and thee,
In the language of thy Muse,
    Have forgot Love's Deity;
They deny to write a line,
    And do onely talk of thine.
        Then lov'd Adonis come away,
        For Friendship brooks not thy Delay.

By thy sweet Althea's voice
    We conjure thee to return;
Or we'l rob thee of that choice
    In whose Flames each Heart would burn;
That inspir'd by her and Sack,
    Such company we will not lack,
        That Poets in the Age to come,
        Shall write of our Elysium.

Ostella; or the Faction of Love and Beauty reconcil'd, 1650

TO MY SELF

SHE is exactly glorious. On her eye
    Lovers may read better Philosophie
    Than E're th'Athenians taught; she's high in Name,
Higher in beauty than the reach of Fame.
But highest in her Virtue and her Mind,
And yet she wants not Nature to be kind,
But ev'n unto the meanest Creature she
Shoots Lustre through a sweet humility.
Shee's great, but yet not greater than my Love,
Nor higher than my Flame: then on, and prove
The temper of her Brest; try if it be
Arm'd against Love, and his Artillery.
But, (oh), I feel my heart consume like fire,
That wasts it self in seeking to aspire.

                              Ibid.

OSTELLA FORTH OF A TOWN:
TO MY HEART

HEART be content, though she be gone,
      Let Reason govern thee:
    Thou hast so much of Pleasure known,
   'Tis fit a season'd Misery
   Should temper thy Prosperity.

Absence doth whet the Appetite,
   Which Presence dull'd before,
There is no Pleasure truly great,
    Nor sweet of such effectual pow'r,
    Till season'd with a little sow'r.

⟨ 197 ⟩

Tatham

> He cannot trule prize Delight,
>   That ne'r knew Misery;
> Nor deem the glory of the Light
>   Untill by wanting it, he be
>   Sensible of its purity.
>
> Think this the time of thy lost health
>   Which when restor'd to thee,
> Ev'n from the Ruine of thy Wealthe
>   It brings a perfect Remedy,
>   To double thy Felicity.

Ibid.

REASON

> REASON and I long time known friends,
>   In all things did comply,
> Till suddenly for unknown ends
>   It shun'd my company.
>
> And whatsoe're I said or did,
>   It still did fly the Sense,
> As though some Sophistry lay hid,
>   Or Errour came from thence.
>
> At last admiring at the Cause
>   Of its so strange Neglect,
> I Conjur'd it by its own Laws,
>   To yield me more respect;
>
> And to resolve me speedily
>   Why we at difference were,
> Since first a solemn League did tie
>   Us to a Sense more fair,
> Knowing I was in Love, it answered me,
>   Reason and Madmen never could agree.

Ibid.

SEEING A LADY

Tatham

O<small>H</small>, she is fair: Fair as the Eastern Morn
    When she is pleas'd the Summer to adorn
    With her Spring's Glory: Sweet as...
Leave, begging-Muse! thy praise gains no Relief,
Since from her glory I derive my grief.

Ibid.

WATKYNS

ROWLAND WATKYNS (*fl.* 1662). A Brecknockshire vicar, who was dispossessed of his living during the Commonwealth and who probably then practised as a physician. He published only one volume of verse, which is full of good poetry, *Flamma sine Fumo: or Poems without Fictions, etc.* 1662. (At the end is a small treatise on medical subjects.) He is a religious poet of considerable distinction, quietly effective in his gentle way.

THE GARDENER

She supposing him to be the Gardener, said unto him. . . .
John 20

MARY prevents the day; she rose to weep,
And see the bed where Jesus lay asleep.
She found out whom she sought, but doth
    not know
Her Master's face; he is the gardener now.
This Gardener Eden's Garden did compose,
For which the chiefest Plants and Flowers he chose.
He took great care to have sweet rivers run
T'enrich the ground, where he his work begun.
He is the Gardener still, and knoweth how
To make the Lillies and the Roses grow.
He knows the time to set, when to remove
His living plants to make them better prove.
He hath his pruning knife, when we grow wild,
To tame our nature, and make us more mild:
He curbs his dearest children when 'tis need:
He cuts his choycest Vines and makes them bleed.
He weeds the poisonous herbs, which clog the
    ground;
He knows the rotten hearts, he knows the sound.

The Blessed Virgin was the pleasant bower   *Watkyns*
This Gardener lodg'd in his appointed hour:
Before his birth his Garden was the womb,
In death he in a Garden chose his Tomb.

Flamma sine Fumo, 1662

THE CHANGES

Tempora mutantur nos et mutamur in illis.

THE painful Bee, which to her hive doth bring
Sweet honey, in her tail retains a sting.
Our sweetest joyes are interlin'd with cares,
No field of corn but hath some choaking tares.
The stream, which doth with silent motion slide
Is oftentimes disturb'd with wind and tide.
Who sits today in Honour's lap and sings,
God soon can change his tune and clip his wings.
Sometimes the Sea doth ebb, and sometimes flow,
Now with, anon against the tide we row;
No haven's so secure but some ill blast
May toss the ship, and break the stately Mast:
Who now in Court doth dance and lift his head,
To morrow droops, and sickly keeps his bed.
The King may beg and beggars may command.
High Cedars fall when little shrubs do stand.
The sweetest comfort I do feel, or find,
Though fortune change, is not to change my mind.

Ibid.

FROM three dark places Christ came forth this day,
First from his Father's bosome, where he lay
Concealed till now; then from the typic Law,
Where we his manhood but by figures saw;
And lastly from his mother's womb he came
To us a perfect God and perfect Man.
Now in a Manger lies th'eternal Word;
The Word he is, yet can no speech afford.
He is the Bread of Life, yet hungry lies,
The living Fountain, yet for drink he cries;
He cannot help, or clothe himself at need,
Who did the Lillies cloath and Ravens feed:
He is the Light of Lights, yet now doth shroud
His glory with our nature as a cloud:
He came to us a little one, that we
Like little children might in malice be;
Little he is, and wrapped in clouts, lest he
Might strike us dead, if clothed with majesty.
Christ had four beds, and those not soft, nor brave,
The Virgin's Womb, the Manger, Cross and Grave.
The Angels sing this day; and so will I
That have more reason to be glad than they.   *Ibid.*

THE MERCIFUL SAMARITANE

No balm from Gilead, no Physitian can
Heal me, but Christ, the true Samaritane.
When I am sick, and when my wounds are foul,
He hath his oyle and wine to clense my soul.
My sins the thieves, which wounded me, have bin;
Help, Lord, conduct me to thy peaceful Inn.   *Ibid.*

SOME fragrant flowers the smell, some trees the sight
Do much content, some pearls are wondrous bright:
There's not so sweet a flower, so fair a tree,
So pure a gemme in all the world, as she:

Some Ladies humble are, and some are wise;
Some chast, some kind, some fair to please the eyes;
All vertues do in her like stars appear,
And make a glorious constellation there.

Ibid.

THE SPRING

SEE how the wanton Spring
    In green is clad,
Hark how the birds do sing,
    I'le not be sad.
Doth not the blushing Rose
    Breath sweet perfume?
I will my spice disclose,
    But not presume.
The dew falls in the grass
    And hastes away,
Which makes me mind my glass
    Which will not stay.
Now plants and herbs do grow
    In every place,
Lord, let me now be slow
    In growth of Grace.

Behold the fruitful trees
And fertil ground;
Observe the painful Bees
Whose hives abound.
I will not barren be
Nor waste my days,
Like sluggards, that are free
From vertuous ways.

Ibid.

THE WISH

Hoc est summum mei, caputque voti.

A LITTLE house, a quiet wife,
Sufficient food to nourish life,
Most perfect health, and free from harm,
Convenient clothes to keepe me warm.
The liberty of foot, and mind,
And grace the ways of God to find.
This is the summe of my desire,
Until I come unto heaven's quire.

Ibid.

UPON THE FAIR AND VERTUOUS GENTLEWOMAN MRS M. S. THAT CAN SING EXCELLENTLY

Gratior est virtus veniens e corpore pulchro.

W HEN first I did this Virgin spie,
The object pleas'd my serious eye:
But when I heard her sing, I swear,
The musick took both heart and ear.
Those inward vertues please us best,
Which are with outward beauty drest;

And 'tis a comely thing to find   *Watkyns*
In bodies fair, a fairer mind:
The Harp, the Viol hither bring,
And Birds, musitians of the Spring;
When she doth sing, those must be mute,
They are but Cymbals to the Lute:
She with her Notes doth rise, and fall,
More sweetly than the Nightingall:
God in her pious heart keeps place,
Some Angel in her voice and face.

Ibid.

THE BIBLE

MUCH books I have perus'd, but I protest
Of books the sacred Bible is the best.
Some books may much of humane Learning
    boast
But here's the language of the Holy Ghost.
Hence we draw living water, here we do
Observe the Patriarchs' lives, and doctrine too:
Here Christ himself directs us how to pray,
And to the Gate of Heaven chalks the way.
Here is the salve which gives the blind their sight,
All darkness to expel; here is the light:
Here is strong meat for men and milk to feed
The weaker babes, which more perfection need;
Cast off erroneous pamphlets, wanton rhymes,
All feigned books of love, which cheat the times,
And read this book of life; those shall appear
With Christ in Heaven which are written here.

Ibid.

THE WEDDING GARMENT

FAITH is the wedding garment, lin'd within
With Love, without foul spots or stains of sin.
Humility is the most decent lace
And patient hope, which doth this garment grace.
Without this royal robe no guest is fit
To sup, or at the Lord's own table sit.

Ibid.

THE HOUR-GLASS

Inter spemque metumque timores inter et iras
Omnem crede diem tibi diluxisse supremum.

OUR time consumes like smoke and posts away,
Nor can we treasure up a month or day.
The sand within the transitory glass
Doth haste, and so our silent minutes pass.
Consider how the lingring hour-glass sends
Sand after sand, until the stock it spends.
Year after year we do consume away
Until our debt to Nature we do pay.
Old age is full of grief: the life of man,
(If we consider), is but like a span
Stretcht from a swollen hand: the more extent
It is by strength, the more the pains augment.
Desire not to live long, but to live well.
How long we live not years, but actions tell.

Ibid.

THE POOR WIDOW'S MITE

Watkyns

OUR Saviour did prefer the Widow's mite
Before the rich men's gifts. God takes delight
More in the heart than hands, and he doth measure
How great our love is, not how much our treasure.
Give all thy full possessions but thy love,
Thy gift will an abomination prove.
Love makes cold water wine, small actions great,
And without love no bounty is compleat.

Ibid.

PROVERBIAL SENTENCES

(*a*) He that hath spice enough within his fist,
His cup of drink may season as he list.

(*b*) Who hath the better game doth fear the end:
Who hath the worse doth hope the game will mend.

(*c*) When I was born I did lament and cry,
And now each day doth show the reason why.

(*d*) Who in the glass doth oft behold her face,
Hath little care to dress her dwelling place.

(*e*) When once the tree is fallen which did stand,
Then every man will take his axe in hand.

(*f*) No Church yard is so hansome anywhere,
As will straight move one to be buried there.

(*g*) Here is great talk of Turk and Pope: but I
Find that my neighbour doth more hurt than they.

Ibid.

WILLAN

LEONARD WILLAN (*fl.* 1649–1670). Playwright, poet and miscellany writer, who enjoyed a reputation in his own day for his all-round, literary abilities. Herrick eulogizes him for the latter in a poem in *Hesperides*, 1648. His two books of verse are *The Phrygian Fabulist*, 1650? and *Astraea, or True Love's Myrrour. A Pastoral*, 1651. He brings to this fable the sly humour which it needs in the telling and he shows a good poetic fancy. It is worthy of the best company.

A CITIE-MOUS AND FIELD-MOUS

A CITIE-MOUS richlie arrai'd,
　　To her Allie's a Progress made.
　　In a Champian seated stood
The Palace of his noble Blood.
Not far from whence encountred him
The Field-Mous, top of all his kin,
Which interviewed he solemnly,
With all due Rites of Cerimonie.
Whence hee conducts him to his Cel,
The Roof whereof was Pimprenel;
The Entrance traced sundrie waies,
(Like to the windings of a Maze),
For strength, not state, was order'd so,
To keepe out raine, or winde, or snow.
Suddenly served was the Feast,
Travel had hunger-stroke our Guest;
A Mushrome spread with Codlin-skin
The Table was and Covering.
A mightie Mess first usher'd came,
Which did all sorts of Puls contein:
Of Wheat, Oat, Pea, Tare, Rie and Rice,
Of Bean, Buck, Barlie, mixt with Spice.

Of sundrie Seeds, contrived so;   *Willan*
This may be called their Oleo.
Next cours, of roots was ordered,
Of Parsnip, Carret, White and Red;
Turnip, Radish, Potato sweet,
Skerret, Oringo, and of Beet;
Som were hatch't, som mince't, som slice't;
And with post ponder all were spice't.
And for their Ragou and Hagou
Were Onions serv'd, and Garlick too.
The Intercours did next succeed,
To urge fresh appetite to feed.
Of Mellon, Pumpion, Cucumber,
Cabbidg, Colwort, and Colli-flour;
Of Thissel-succors hatched small
Which were well pepper'd with Fusball.
Their Liquor from a Christal stream
They had whereon ne'r shined Beam.
In which for Amber-Greece of Musk,
Infused was in Acorn-husk
A Pearl of Dew, or elf of Hail,
As Heat or Moisture did prevail.
The Deser, hereto closure put's;
Of Wall, of Hair, of Hassel-nuts:
Of Pears and Apples, Plums and Cheries,
Dew, Straw, Raspe, Mull, Bill and Black-
    berries.
Of Medler, Service, Corn, they fed,
Of Grapes and Currens, white and red;
But of Beech, Oak, Thorn, Bramble-Maste
They far more sparingly did taste.
The Grashopper, the Gnat, the Bee,
In Consort were their Minstralsie.

Willan   The Citie-Mous, the Feast thus past,
Soberly seemed to distaste
The meanness of the Countrie fare;
Boasting the Citie's to be rare.
That which might bee no vapour thought,
The Field-Mous hee to Citie brought;
Where in a Store-hous hee beheld
Such Dainties, as there most excel'd:
Here a Custard, there a Tart,
Of a fat Capon there a part;
Here a Gammon stuft with cloves;
There did a Pie Red-Dear inclose;
Here Pheasant, Partridge, Woodcock, Quail;
There Knot, Snipe, Tiel, Turtle and Rail;
Spice, Sugar, Suckets wet and drie,
Were all disperst confusedly:
Whereof so eagerly both fed,
Order was none distinguished.
E're long, i'th dore ratled a keie,
Which scar'd both Host and Guest awaie.
The Field-Mous who her cours forgot,
For haste fell in a Honie-pot,
Which being nigh full, and candi'd o're,
Bemired much, hee got to shore.
Thence in a Barrel skipt of Sope,
Whence he escaped by a Rope;
The Balance fastned to the Scale,
From thence hee rusht into a Frale
Of Raisins, which, strugling therein,
His clammie Coat stript from his skin.
Thence to a hole, where both remain,
Till they came in went out again.
Then issued out the Citie-Mous,

Frisking with joie about the hous,   *Willan*
While the poor Field-Mous there with dread
Remained trembling, almost dead.
'Til him the Citie-Mous invites
Again to taste of his Delights;
Assuring him the peril o're.
Out snekt the Field-Mous, yet forbore
To feed; jealous surpriz'd to bee,
Asking the Citie-Mous if hee
Were often thus assaulted; who
With confidence replied thereto,
"Each hour, each hour. Custom makes light
Where that is weightie wants fore-sight."
The Field-Mous, much amazed, cried,
"Was ever sens so stupified!
With my mean Cates, I rest secur'd;
Rest thou with dang'rous sweets immur'd."

Moral

The humble, calm, and innocent estate,
This of a countrie life doth intimate.
Whose sober temper onely thus relies
On what successfull Industrie supplies.
While Citie lives, their riot to support,
Make Rapine, Fraud and Violence a sport:
With whose Alarums hourly pursued;
So oft their lusts, so oft are griefs renew'd.

The Phrygian Fabulist, 1650?

WYVILL

SIR CHRISTOPHER WYVILL (1614–1681). A baronet of Yorkshire who wrote a treatise against popery and a collection of verses. The latter was *Certaine Serious Thoughts, etc.* 1647.

GOING TO BED

A PRAYER

THOU sacred Arbiter of life and death,
    Who summon'st, at thy pleasure, vitall breath,
    When in thy house my elevated soule
Should mount to thee, yet lingring here, doth foule
Her self with terrene fancies, make mine eye
Recall my thoughts and preach mortality.
There lye those dear remembrancers I have,
Two parents, and two children in one grave.
In twice two yeares thy wisdome saw it best
To call these two sweet couples to their rest.
And since so neer on both sides I have seen
Thine arrowes to me, teach me how to weane
From this distemper'd globe my mis-plac'd love
And fix it firmly on the things above.
Then, if't shall please thee next to call on mee,
I'le boldly leave this clay and come to thee.

Certaine Serious Thoughts, etc. 1647

ANONYMOUS POEMS

TWO EPITAPHS from Burford Church, Gloucester. The first is dated 1668. The opening lines are full of charm. The second is earlier and may have been written by Lady Tanfield herself.

EPITAPH

ON A TOMB IN BURFORD CHURCH, GLOUCESTER

Lo, Hudled up, together lye
Gray Age, Grene Youth, white Infancy.
If Death doth Nature's Laws dispence,
And reconciles all difference,
'Tis fit, one Flesh one house should have
One Tombe, one epitaph, one Grave;
And they that liv'd and lov'd each other
Should dye and lye and sleep together.
So Reader whether go or stay
Thou must not hence be long away.

ANON.

Burford Church

EPITAPH

LADY TANFIELD UPON HER HUSBAND

Here shadows lie,
    Whilst life is sadd,
Still hopes to die,
    To him she hadd.
In bliss is hee
    Whom I lov'd best;
Thrice happy shee
    With him to rest.

⟨ 213 ⟩

So shall I be
  With him I loved;
And hee with me
  And both us blessed.
Love made me Poet,
  And this I writ;
My harte did doe yt
  And not my witt.

ANON.?

Burford Church

AN ELEEGY

ON THE DEATH OF A SCHOOLE-MASTER

This comes from a printed book, *Poems, consisting of Epistles and Epigrams. By John Eliot*, 1658. Many other poems in the book can be traced to other poets of the period, and it is quite uncertain whether John Eliot himself wrote this delightful tribute.

MUST he dye thus? has an eternall sleep
    Seiz'd on each Muse that it can't sing nor
      weep?
Had he no friends? no merits? or no purse
To purchase mourning? Or had he that curse
Which has the scraping Worldling still frequented,
To live unlov'd and perish unlamented.
    No, none of these; but in this Atlas' fall
Learning for present found its funerall.
Nor was't for want of grief, but scope and vent,
Not sullenness, but strong, deep astonishment.
Small griefs are but soon wept out, great ones come
With bulk, and strike the straight lamenters dumb.
    This was the scoolemaster that did derive
    From parts and piety's prerogative:
The glory of that good but painfull art
Who had high learning but an humble heart:
The Drake of Grammer learning, whose great pain
Circled that Globe, and made that voyage plain.
    Time was, when th'artless paedagogue did stand,
With his vimineous scepter in his hand
Raging like Bajazet or'e the 'tugging fry,
Who though unhors'd were not of th'infantry;
Applying, like a glister, hic, haec, hoc,
Till the poor Lad's beat to a whipping block;

And hold so long to know a verb and noun
Till each had Propria maribus of's own:
As if not fit to learn As in Praesenti
But legally, when they were one and twenty.
Those few that went to th'Universitys then
Went with deliberation, and were men.
Nor were our Academies in those dayes
Fill'd with Chuck-farthing Batchelours and boyes
But schollers with more Beard and age went hence,
Then our new lapwing-Lectrers skip from thence.

     By his industrious labour now we see
Boys coated borne to th'Universitie
Who suck'd in Latin, and did scorn to seek
Their scourge and top in English but in Greek.
Hebrew the general puzzler of old heads,
Which the gray Dunce with pricks and comments
  reads
And dubs himselfe a schollar by it, grew
As naturall t'him as if he'd been a Jew.

     But above all he timely did inspire
His Children's breasts with an aetheriall fire.
And sanctifi'd their early Learning so,
That they in grace as they in wit did grow.

     Yet nor his grace nor learning could defend him,
From that mortality that did attend him.
Nor can there now be any difference known
Between his learned bones and those with none.
For that grand Lev'ler death hudles t'one place
Rich, poor, wise, foolish, noble and the base.

     This only is our comfort and defence,
He was not immaturely ravish'd hence.
But to our benefit, and to his own
Undying fame and honour, let alone,

Till he had finish'd what he was to do,   *Anonymous*
Then naturally split himselfe in two.   *Poems*
    And that's one cause he had so few moyst eyes,
He made men learned, and that made them wise
And overrule their passions, since they see
Tears would but show their own infirmity.
And 'tis but loving madness to deplore
The fate of him that shall be seen no more.
But only I cropt in my tender yeares,
Without or tongue, or wit, but sighs and Tears:
And yet I come to offer what is mine,
An immolation to his honour'd shrine.
And retribute what he confer'd on me
Either to's person or his memorie.
Rest pious soul and let that happie grave
That us entrusted with thy Relicks, have
This just inscription, that it holds the dust
Of one that was Wise, learned, pious, just.

ANON.

Poems, consisting of Epistles and Epigrams.
By John Eliot, 1658

EPITAPH

IN MEMORYE OF THE FIVE CHILDREN OF
WILLIAM AND ANNE AUSTIN

This may have been written by William Austin (1587–1624),
who was a considerably known poet.

READER,
　When thou knowst in this Urne
　　Five infants doe sojourne,
Thinke long thou canst not burne
When sutch new flames doe turne
　　　So soone to shade.
For I, whoe live to read
Heer half my boughs lye dead,
Larne, if sutch branches dye,
The stock maye by and by,
Wither at Roote, and fade.

Yet call not this their tombe,
Rather their mother's Wombe,
Where when their god doth come
To give us all our doome
　　　They shall arise
New borne, full, perfect men,
Licke to their judge, and then
Wee that did for them weep
Shall see they did but sleep
To grow and mock our eyes.

ANON.

Harley MS. 3910

MY WISHES

From a very rare printed book, *Eliza's Babes: or the Virgin's-Offering, etc.* 1652. It seems unworthy of the complete oblivion which has fallen, as it was sure to fall, upon a book of verse with such a title.

I WISH no wit to wrong my Brother,
I wish not wealth to wrong another;
I wish no beauty to enthrall,
I wish no worldly wish at all.
I wish from sin God would me bring,
I wish for heaven at my ending.

ANON.

Eliza's Babes: or The Virgin's-Offering, etc. 1652

A SHORT GLOSSARY

OF DIFFICULT WORDS AND REFERENCES

Amber-Greece of Musk (page 209, line 19).   Ambergris: a grey,
   odorous substance used in perfumery. Amber-seed is Musk-
   seed. Fr. *ambre gris*, "grey amber". The spellings "Greece" and
   "Grease" came in at the beginning of the seventeenth century,
   when people were trying to explain the origin of the "gris".

Bajazet (p. 215, l. 21).   This is a reference to Bajazid, or Bajasid
   (1347–1403), who was Sultan of the Turks from 1389–1403. He
   typifies here an Eastern tyrant. The historical Bajazid conquered
   Bulgaria and a large part of Asia Minor. He was defeated by
   Timur at Angora in 1402, and held prisoner by him until his
   death. There was a tradition that Timur carried him about from
   city to city in an iron cage. This alleged ill-treatment forms the
   most powerful portion of Marlowe's *Tamberlane*, and also of
   Rowe's *Tamerlane*. In the former play he is shown on the stage
   in an iron cage and fed with scraps. His name would have been
   well known to most seventeenth-century readers.

Bengewine (p. 147, l. 5).   This is probably a spelling for "Ben-
   jamin", a gum benzoin or balsam. Perhaps the printer has "w"
   for "m". Ben Jonson's name in Henslowe is spelt "Bengemen".
   Cf. Herrick, *Hesperides*, 1648:
   > "Leave a name as sweet
   > As Benjamin and Storax when they meet."

Botchy-Lazer (p. 144, l. 20).   Botchy means "covered with botches,
   or excrescences". Botch, O.Fr. *boche* O.N.Fr., O.Fr. *boce*. Cf.
   Troilus and Cressida, II, i, 6:
   > "were not that a botchy core?"
   Lazer from "Lazarus" in the biblical story.

Breeme (p. 141, l. 16).   Breme, now poetic and dialect only. It
   means here "fierce", "raging". It is used of the sea. Cf. Dray-
   ton, *Heroic Epistles*, 1598, XVI, 8:
   > "On whose breeme sea the Icie Mountaines flote."

Glossary Cade (p. 3, l. 24). Young one, cadet. The origin of this word is unknown. Cf. the will of Jane Lovet, 1551: "Three Cade lambes that go abowte the house."

Calamite (p. 147, l. 5). A variety of hornblende. It is used here simply to indicate the crystal-like pieces of resinous storax.

Capapee (p. 71, l. 6). Cap-à-pie. Fr. *cap-à-pied*, "From head to foot".

Cassia (p. 147, l. 7). A genus of plants of many species, including senna and laurel, the bark of which is used in medicine.

Cauls (p. 38, l. 11). A caul is a thin membrane. It is usually used either of the membrane which covers the lower intestine or of that which protects the head of some children at birth.

Champian (p. 208, l. 3). This is a variant of "champaign". It was much more usual than the latter form in the seventeenth century.

Cicuta (p. 102, l. 19). Hemlock.

Cimmerian (p. 101, l. 30). The Cimmerii were a mythical people mentioned by Homer. They were supposed to dwell in the farthest west, enveloped in constant mists and darkness. Cimmerian time may mean "a time of darkness" because Henry is dead. The historical Cimmerii were wanderers and perhaps the poet refers to them also. The meaning of the passage is a little obscure, but it seems to be that as a Pharos, or light-house, guides wanderers, so the tomb he would build for Henry would guide all wanderers on earth to Heaven.

Cocker (p. 133, l. 8). Indulge, pamper. The origin is obscure, but cf. Du. *kokelen*, "to nourish, foster".

Codlin (p. 208, l. 17). A cooking apple.

Cop (p. 78, l. 10). Tuft, sheaf, crest on a bird. O.N. *koppr*, "a cup".

Culver (p. 100, l. 17). A wood pigeon.

Daphnis (p. 148, l. 29). Now called Daphne. This is the evergreen shrub, named from the nymph Daphne who was changed by her father into a laurel-tree when Apollo was pursuing her.

Davour (p. 41, l. 1). To fade, droop, wither. This is a dialect word, Devon, Cornwall, Somerset and Wiltshire. It rhymes with "waver". Devon: "The flowers be daver'd a'ready."

Delius (p. 37, l. 1). Delius was the surname of the god Apollo, from the isle of Delos. The myth tells how the latter was a floating isle until Zeus fastened it by adamantine chains to the bottom of the sea, that it might be a secure resting place for Leto (Latona) for the birth of Apollo and Artemis. A Delian was an inhabitant of this floating isle.

Dyll (p. 149, l. 6). Dill, a plant not unlike fennel.

Engastranith (p. 159, l. 3). This is a form of the modern "Engastrimyth", one who appears to speak in the belly, a ventriloquist. The word occurs in Sylvester's *Du Bartas* (1698, I, ii).

Fistula (p. 147, l. 7.) This means "reed" or "pipe" and refers to the shape of one species of cassia.

Frie (p. 75, l. 19). A crowd of young fish just spawned, offspring, young children. O.N. *frio*. Cf. *Macbeth*, IV, ii, 83:

> "What you Egge?
> Yong fry of Treachery."

Fusball (p. 209, l. 16). Fuzzball, a puff-ball.

Germander (p. 149, l. 11). A genus of plant, especially the blue-flowered speedwell.

Hagou (p. 209, l. 9). This is almost certainly "haggis", the famous dish of Scotland. It is an old form, probably dialect. Cf. haggus, hagws, etc.

Hazzard (p. 143, l. 24). This is the name given in the game of tennis to each of the winning openings in the tennis-court. The "hazard" side is that side of the court into which the ball is served. Cf. *Henry V*, I, ii, 263:

> "We will in France...play a set,
> Shall strike his fathers Crowne into the hazard."

Hougon Mess (p. 119, l. 22). This probably refers to "Huguenote" (Fr.), a kitchen stove, and hence to "Des œufs à la Huguenote", eggs cooked or poached in mutton gravy.

Isop (p. 149, l. 11). Hyssop, an aromatic herb.

Knot (p. 210, l. 14). A wading bird of the snipe family, named after King Canute (Knut), who was very fond of it.

Lungwort (p. 149, l. 27). A purple-flowered herb, with leaves spotted like lungs.

Mace (p. 147, l. 4).   A spice. It is formed from the dried, outer seed of the nutmeg.

Marjorum (p. 149, l. 6).   Marjoram, an aromatic plant.

Medway Cowslips (p. 148, l. 15).   The district round Maidstone and the Medway is famed to-day for its Spring flowers. Cf. Bluebell Hill.

Mislyn (p. 15, l. 21).   Mixed. Cf. maslin, meslin.

Oleo (p. 209, l. 2).   Olio: a medley or mixture. The *olus* of Horace, a potherb, or a mixture of herbs, etc.

Oringo (p. 209, l. 6).   This is undoubtedly a corrupt or misspelt form of "eryngo", a candied root of the sea-holly. It was formerly used as a sweetmeat, and was regarded as an aphrodisiac. Cf. *The Merry Wives of Windsor*, v, v, 23: "Let it...haile kissing Comfits and snow Eringoes." Cf. Marston, *Scourge of Villanie*, 1, iii, 181: "Now, Sophie, Ringoes eate."

Pharos (p. 101, l. 27).   A lighthouse built by Ptolemy II on the small isle of Pharos, off the coast of Egypt. It became the general name in literature of the period for a lighthouse.

Post ponder (p. 209, l. 8).   Is this connected with "panada", bread boiled to pulp and flavoured? It seems better to change "ponder" to "pouder", which is probably the correct reading. "Post" then means "poppy-head or opium". It is flavoured with "poppy-seed powder".

Powt (p. 73, l. 8).   Pout, poult, young chick. Fr. *poule*. It is especially used of a young partridge.

Pucillage (p. 133, l. 2).   Cf. Fr. *pucelage*, "maidenhead, virginity". This word is coined from the French by the poet.

Ragou (p. 209, l. 9).   Ragout, a highly-seasoned stew.

Rail (p. 210, l. 14).   A wading-bird.

Rotchets (p. 72, l. 2).   Rochets, linen outer garments.

Sallet-budded (p. 149, l. 19).   A sallet was a light helmet, and the word here refers to the shape of the broom buds.

Service (p. 209, l. 27).   The pear-like fruit of the service tree.

Skerret (p. 209, l. 6).   Skirret, a species of water-parsnip, which was formerly very much cultivated in Europe for its esculent tubers. Cf. 1639 Horn and Rob. *Gate Lang. Unl.* XIII, par. 126: "The rape...the navew, parsnip, carret, skirwit...."

Smaragdine (p. 102, l. 1).   Smaragdite is an emerald green mineral which is sometimes called diallage.

Spicknard (p. 147, l. 6).   Spikenard, the Indian perfume, or unguent prepared from the plant.

Spittle (p. 127, l. 11).   Spittoon.

Storax (p. 147, l. 5).   A sweet-smelling resin, which is used in medicine as a stimulant.

Sucket (p. 210, l. 15).   Sweetmeat.

Sullibub (p. 75, l. 17).   This is usually spelt "syllabub". It was a drink made of wine and milk which was very popular during the seventeenth century.

Theanthropos (p. 182, l. 8).   The Gk. "theos" and "anthropos". Someone who was both divine and human.

Thessalian herb (p. 149, l. 7).   This is "thyme", which is constantly referred to among the classical poets as growing upon Olympus, Ossa, etc.

Thissel-succors (p. 209, l. 15).   Suckers, or sweet, young shoots of the thistle, which mice would enjoy.

Tiel (p. 210, l. 14).   Teal; a web-footed water-fowl, nearly allied to the common duck.

Toutsain (p. 149, l. 21).   Tutsan, St John's Wort, which was then used to heal wounds. Fr. *toutesaine*, "all sound", "healed".

Truckman (p. 128, l. 26).   To "truck", traffic, hawk, bargain.

Zone (p. 119, l. 28).   A girdle worn round the body. It was a symbol of virginity.

Zoophyte (p. 138, l. 1).   A living, plant-like animal, as sea-anemones, sponges, jellyfish.

INDEX OF AUTHORS

INDEX OF FIRST LINES

⟨ **229** ⟩

⟨ 231 ⟩

⟨ 233 ⟩

For EU product safety concerns, contact us at Calle de José Abascal, 56–1°, 28003 Madrid, Spain or eugpsr@cambridge.org.

www.ingramcontent.com/pod-product-compliance
Ingram Content Group UK Ltd.
Pitfield, Milton Keynes, MK11 3LW, UK
UKHW020318140625
459647UK00018B/1923